TJE

KIDS' KNITS
and crochet

CONTENTS

EDITORIAL
Managing Editor: Judy Poulos
Editorial Co-ordinator: Margaret Kelly
Editorial Assistant: Ella Martin
U.K. Consultant: Norma Lane

GARMENT DESIGN
Fusako Burton

DESIGN AND PRODUCTION
Margie Mulray
Chris Hatcher

PHOTOGRAPHY
Jon Waddy
Styling: Sally Hirst

DESIGN AND PRODUCTION MANAGER
Nadia Sbisa

PUBLISHER
Philippa Sandall

Kids' Knits and Crochet
ISBN 1 86343 007 5

Family Circle is a registered trademark of
IPC Magazines Ltd.
Published by J.B. Fairfax Press Ltd by
arrangement with IPC Magazines Ltd.

Formatted by J.B. Fairfax Press Pty Ltd
Output by Adtype, Sydney
Printed by Toppan Printing Co, Hong Kong

Distributed by J.B. Fairfax Press Ltd
9 Trinity Centre, Park Farm Estate
Wellingborough, Northants, U.K.
Tel: (0933) 402330
Fax: (0933) 402234

*T*raditional charm with a very up-to-date flair. You will find all this and more in our collection of KIDS' KNITS AND CROCHET.

We've designed a rainbow of jumpers and cardigans, all in pure wool, that will be a pleasure to knit or crochet and to wear. Your little ones are sure to love the bright colours, fun motifs and, most especially, the cuddly toys. There's a menagerie of cuddly animals, as well as a group of very elegant dolls from all around the world.

If you are a regular donor to the church bazaar or school fete, or have a multitude of young relatives to remember at Christmas time, then this is the book for you! The toys require so little yarn that you can even use up all those scraps that we knitters hoard for just such a 'rainy day'.

We've deliberately chosen styles with a timeless appeal that you will never tire of. This book is certain to become a favourite that you'll enjoy going back to year after year.

For each of the garments you will also find the correct knitting or crochet tension is given. This is not the case for the toys where absolutely accurate tension is not quite so important. Through the book you will find all the useful information you will need to ensure a perfect finish. There are hints on finishing, pressing and making up the final product, as well as a special Knitting Class and Crochet Class to turn even a beginner into a confident craftsperson.

TOY SAFETY

Choose materials and trims appropriate to the age of the child for whom you are making the toy. For children under the age of three years do not use buttons and beads for eyes on toys. They are too easily pulled off and can become a serious hazard. For toys for very little ones embroider on the eyes instead.

All our patterns are graded so that you can choose a pattern that is just right for you to make.

beginners

average skills

experienced

METRIC / IMPERIAL CONVERSION CHART

METRIC	INCHES
2 mm	$1/16$
6 mm	$1/4$
1 cm	$3/8$
2.5 cm	1
5 cm	2
30 cm	12
91 cm	36

GETTING STARTED
MATERIALS
If you change from the recommended ply yarn for any reason, it will affect the size and shape of your garment. If you must change, knit a tension square before you begin.

Yarn quantities given with each pattern are approximate as the actual quantity needed varies so much from person to person. If you can return unused yarn to the shop, it is often better to buy an extra ball to ensure that you are able to complete your garment or toy in yarn from the same dye lot.

SIZES
Garments are given in two, three or four sizes. In each case the instructions for the smallest size are given first and the instructions for the other sizes appear in brackets. Where there is no figure or a nought (0) is given for a particular size this indicates that no stitches or rows are to be worked for that size. Where only one number is shown, it applies to all sizes.

Rather than give the garment sizes by age we prefer to describe sizes in terms of body and garment measurements. This is because there can clearly be quite a difference in the sizes of two children of exactly the same age.

TENSION OR GAUGE
Correct tension is crucial to the success of a knit or crochet garment. It is disappointing to spend so many hours and so much money on yarn, only to find that the finished garment looks nothing like the picture and doesn't fit the way it should. Taking a little time at the beginning to knit a tension square will be time very well spent and will avoid that disappointment. Read all about tension, what it is, how to measure it and how to keep tension correct on page 23.

PRESSING
Plain knitting usually looks best if it is pressed but whether you press or not depends on the type of yarn you are using and the pattern you have chosen. Always check the ball band on your yarn for any special instructions. Remember that, in order to retain its elasticity, ribbing is never pressed.

Knitting is usually pressed on the wrong side, using a damp cloth and suitable iron temperature. Take care not to push the iron to and fro as you go, as this tends to stretch the fabric and distort the shape. Simply place the iron on the piece and lift it straight off.

BLOCKING
Blocking involves the pinning into shape of a piece of knitting or crochet on a flat, padded surface before it is lightly sprayed with water and left to dry in shape.

JOINING PIECES
It is important to assemble your knitting and crochet neatly for a professional finish. There are a number of methods of joining pieces, of which the two described are the most commonly used. The backstitch method is the most popular because it is quite simple and provides a strong seam. To use this method, place the two pieces together, with right sides facing, and backstitch them together one stitch in from the edge. Take care to match any pattern in the two pieces and to avoid

pulling the stitches too tightly.

The second method of joining pieces is the 'edge-to-edge' method. It produces a less bulky seam than the back-stitch method, which makes it ideal for lighter yarns, baby clothes, lacy patterns and attaching bands. To join pieces using this method, place them edge-to-edge, right sides up. Again it is important to match patterns and rows on the two pieces. Securing the yarn to the lower edge of the left-hand piece, pick up the loop between the first and second stitches on the first row of that piece, then pick up the same loop on the right hand piece. Working upwards in this way, complete sewing the seam, taking care not to pull it too tightly.

FINISHING OFF
When you have pressed and joined your pieces, it is a good idea to darn or weave in all the loose ends for a really neat finish. Leaving a tail of about 12 cm (5 in) when you break off the yarn makes this job a lot easier. If you are using very thick yarn it is often a good idea to fray the end and weave each strand in separately.

KNITTING CLASS
GETTING STARTED
There are basically two simple methods of casting on your first row of loops, one using one needle and a thumb and the other using two needles. Which method you choose depends on which you find the most comfortable to use as both work equally well.

Having cast on the required number of stitches you are ready to begin knitting in either purl or knit (plain) stitches. All knitting is basically a combination of these two simple stitches and their arrangement determines the look and feel of the work. The most common pattern, stocking stitch, is worked by working all knit stiches on one (the right) side and all purl stitches on the other (wrong) side of the piece.

INCREASING
The simplest way to increase is to make two stitches out of one, by working into the back and front of the same stitch. Ideally you should try to do this one or two stitches in from the edges for a smooth finish.

You can achieve a virtually invisible increase, anywhere on the row, by making a stitch out of the loop that lies between two stitches on the left needle.

To increase a larger number of stitches at the edges of a piece of knitting, you should cast on the required number of stitches at the beginning of two consecutive rows.

DECREASING
The simplest way of decreasing a stitch is to work two stitches together as though they were one. Again you will achieve a neater look if you do this a stitch or two in from the edge. To decrease a large number of stitches at the edges of your knitting, simply cast them off.

CASTING OR BINDING OFF
To cast off plain knitting (either knitwise or purlwise) simply work the first two stitches in the way prescribed (either knit or purl) and then slip the first of those stitches over the second one. Work the next stitch in the same way and continue to do so until all stitches (or the number required) are cast off.

To cast off in rib work each stitch as it appears on the needle before slipping it off.

JOINING IN YARN

It is always best to join in a new yarn at the edges of a piece of knitting and not in the middle of a row, except of course, if you are knitting a picture knit. Don't knot the ends together but simply leave a length about 12 cm (5 in) long to be darned in later.

If you must join in a new yarn in the centre of a row, use the double strand method where you work the last stitch in the old yarn and let that fall to the back of the work. Leaving a tail about 5 cm (2 in) long, knit the next stitch with the new yarn. For the next three or four stitches use the new yarn doubled and then darn in the tail of the old yarn on the wrong side.

KNITTING WITH COLOURS

Multi-coloured knitting looks great. It can be as simple as working in stripes or as complex as picture knitting. For simple stripes that are quite narrow you can change yarns at one edge and carry the unused one up the side. Similarly if colours have to be carried across a row, providing it is not further than about five stitches, they can be carried across the back of the work. If there are more than five stitches or more than three colours to be carried, you will need to weave the unused yarn through the back of your work or, even better, use separate balls of yarn for each block of colour. Knitting bobbins, available from yarn shops, are ideal for holding these small quantities of yarn and keeping them free of tangles.

The most important rule in multi-coloured knitting is to twist the old yarn with the new one carefully at each change of colour to prevent holes. Remember to darn in all the loose ends on the wrong side before joining the pieces.

CROCHET CLASS
GETTING STARTED

Crochet is worked with a single hook, usually held in the right hand while the left hand controls the tension and feeding of the yarn. Most crochet work begins with a row of foundation chain, a bit like the cast-on row of knitting.

Once you have your foundation or base chain, work back along it using whichever of the crochet stitches your pattern prescribes. To do this, work into a chain one, two, three, four or five chains from the beginning. These missed chains at the beginning of the row curve upwards like a ladder, adding the height that is necessary for the next row to stand. How many chains you miss depend on the stitch you are using and therefore the height you will need to work the next row. Generally you will need to miss one chain for double crochet, two for half treble, three for treble and so on. Remember though, you

may need to experiment to find the exact number that is just right for you, your pattern, yarn and hook size. The missed chain counts as the first stitch on the next row.

TENSION

Correct and even tension is very important for crochet. For right handers it is the left hand which controls the tension. This is easier to do if you keep your left thumb and middle finger close to the hook.

To keep your crochet fabric soft and flexible, take care not to pull the loops too tightly. This is quite simple to do if you make the last loop on the hook much bigger than the preceding ones. In this way, when you complete the stitch you can gently adjust the size of the loop to keep the work loose and supple.

WORKING IN ROWS

At the end of each row you will need to turn and work back along the row, working on the wrong side of the stitches in that row and just to the left of them.

Just as you need to allow for the height at the beginning by missing a chain or two, you will need to allow for the same height at the end of each row. You can do this by working a number of turning chain. The turning chain can also count as the first stitch on the next row. The last stitch of each row is worked into two loops of the last chain to avoid holes.

WORKING IN ROUNDS

Crochet can also be worked in rounds rather than rows, working on the right side of the fabric and making each stitch just to the **right** of the stitch on the previous row. Rounds are generally joined by working a slip stitch into two loops of the chain below.

INCREASING AND DECREASING

Shaping a piece of crochet is done by increasing or decreasing the number of stitches on a row or round. The simplest method of increasing is to work two stitches into one stitch. Generally the instructions will tell you where in the row you should increase and how often.

The specific way of decreasing depends on which stitch you are using. In general terms, decrease by working one stitch where previously there were two. For example, in single crochet, make a loop in each of the next two stitches so that you have loops on your hook. Draw the yarn through both loops on the hook, making one stitch out of two.

CORRECTING MISTAKES

Even the most experienced occasionally make mistakes and its really quite easy to correct them. Simply remove your hook and allow your work to unravel down to the mistake, thereby removing it. Then just pick up where you are and keep on going.

FASTENING OFF

To fasten off your work and to ensure that it is secure, break off the yarn leaving a tail about 12 cm (5 in) long. Using your hook draw this tail through the last loop on the hook and pull it firmly but not tightly. When the piece is complete darn the tail into the back of the work. Do not tie knots.

Nautical Knits

Out on the ocean wave or having fun on the shore this smart twosome are definitely in command in their matching sailor suits. Now if they only had a ship!

SAILOR SUIT WITH CROCHET SKIRT OR PANTS

JUMPER
BACK

With 4.00 mm (No. 8) needles and A, cast on 56 (62, 68) sts. Work in st st. Work 16 rows, then cast on 6 sts at beg of next 2 rows for Side Vents. 68 (74, 80) sts. Cont in st st until work measures 16 (18, 21) cm [6¼ (7, 8¼) in] from beg, ending with WS row. Adjust length at this point if required*.

Shape armholes

Cast/bind off 3 (4, 4) sts at beg of next 2 rows. Dec 1 st at each end of next and every foll 2nd row until 50 (54, 60) sts rem. Work 19 (23, 27) rows straight, ending with WS row.

Shape shoulders and neck

1st row: Cast/bind off 6 (5, 7) sts, knit until 13 (15, 15) sts on right hand needle, cast/bind off centre 12 (14, 16) sts, knit to end. Cont on last 19 (20, 22) sts. Cast/bind off at beg of next and each alt row 6 (5, 7) sts once, 5 (6, 6) sts twice for Shoulder AT SAME TIME dec 1 st at neck edge on 1st 3 rows for all sizes, then work 2 rows straight.

Ret to rem sts, rejoin A at neck edge, dec 1 st at neck edge on 1st 3 rows, then work 2 rows straight AT SAME TIME cast/bind off at beg of every 2nd row 5 (6, 6) sts twice.

FRONT

Work as Back to *.

Shape armholes and divide for V neck

1st row: Cast/bind off 3 (4, 4) sts, knit until 31 (33, 36) sts on right hand needle, TURN.

Cont on these 31 (33, 36) sts. Dec 1 st at neck edge on next and every foll 3rd row until 9 (10, 11) times in all AT SAME TIME dec 1 st at armhole edge on every 2nd row 6 times in all for all sizes.

Cont straight at armhole edge and dec at neck edge as given until 16 (17, 19) sts rem. Cont straight for 6 (7, 8) rows, ending at armhole edge.

Shape shoulder

Cast/bind off at beg of next and every foll 2nd row 6 (5, 7) sts once, 5 (6, 6) sts twice. Ret to rem sts, rejoin A at centre front and finish to match other side.

MATERIALS
Yarn:

For Jumper: 8 ply pure wool crepe 50 g (2 oz balls): 4 (4½, 5) balls white (A); 1 (1, 1) ball navy (B); small quantity of red (C)

For Skirt: 1½ (2, 2) balls white (A); 3 (3½, 4) balls navy (B)

For Pants: 3½ (4, 4½) balls navy (B)

Notions: One pair each 4.00 (4) mm (No. 8) and 3.25 (3¼) mm (No. 10) knitting needles; one each of 4.00 (4) mm (No. 8) and 3.00 (3) mm (No. 11) crochet hooks; elastic for waist; 2 buttons for skirt only

TENSION

Jumper and Pants: 22 sts and 32 rows to 10 cm (4 in) over st st using 4.00 mm (No. 8) needle.

Skirt: 17 tr to 10 cm (4 in) and 8 rows of tr to 9 cm (3½ in) using 4.00 mm (No. 8) hook.

It is important to knit a tension square and to work to the stated tension in order to obtain the required measurements. If your square is bigger use finer needles. If your square is smaller use thicker needles.

NOTE

(1 dc, 2 ch) at beg of tr row stands for 1 tr, and always work the last tr in top of (1 dc, 2 ch)

0 means there are no stitches to be worked for that size

MEASUREMENTS
Jumper:

To fit underarm	51 (56, 61) cm	
	20 (22, 24) in	
Garment measures		
	59 (64, 69) cm	
	23 (25, 27) in	
Length	30 (33, 37) cm	
	11¾ (13, 14½) in	
Sleeve seam	20 (23, 28) cm	
	8 (9, 11) in	

Skirt:

To fit waist	51 (54, 57) cm
	20 (21½, 22½) in
Length	23 (28, 31) cm
	9 (11, 12) in

Pants:

To fit hips	56 (61, 66) cm
	22 (24, 26) in
Outside leg length	
	47 (52, 61) cm
	18½ (20½, 24½) in

SPECIAL ABBREVIATIONS

TrB = treble back: insert hook from back of work, then to left of next st and to back of work, and work 1 tr around stem of st

TrF = treble front: insert hook from front of work, then to left of next st and to front of work, and work 1 tr round the stem of the st

Dec 1 tr = (yoh, insert hook in next st, yoh and draw through, yoh and draw through 2 lps on hook) twice, yoh and draw through 3 lps on hook

Trims for lower edge and side vents

With RS facing, 3.25 mm (No. 10) needles and A, pick up and knit 1 st in each of cast-on sts at lower edge at same time evenly inc 4 sts along row. 60 (66, 72) sts. Knit 9 rows, inc 1 st at each end of 1st row, then on every foll 2nd row 5 times in all. Cast/bind off. With RS facing, 3.25 mm (No. 10) needles and A, pick up 12 sts on side edge between lower corner and cast-on edge for vent. Knit 9 rows, inc 1 st at lower edge on 1st row, and every foll 2nd row 5 times in all. Cast/bind off. Work same on other side vent. Join Trims tog to form corners.

SLEEVES

With 3.25 mm (No. 10) needles and B, cast on 31 (33, 35) sts. Knit 4 rows. Change to A and knit 4 rows. Change to B and knit 8 rows, inc 6 sts on last row. 37 (39, 41) sts. Change to 4.00 mm (No. 8) needles, st st and A only. Inc 1 st each end of 7th row once, then on every foll 6th row until there are 53 (57, 61) sts. Cont straight on these sts until work meas 20 (23, 28) cm [8 (9, 11) in] from beg, or length required, ending with WS row.

Shape top

Cast/bind off 3 (4, 4) sts at beg of next 2 rows. Dec 1 st each end of next 7 rows, then dec 1 st each end of every foll 2nd row 5 times, purl 1 row, then dec 1 st each end of next 6 rows. Cast/bind off.

COLLAR

With 4.00 mm (No. 8) needles, B, cast on 44 (48, 54) sts. Work in st st until piece is 8 (9, 10) cm [3 (3½, 4) in] from beg, ending with WS row.

Divide for neck

1st row: K16 (17, 19) sts, cast/bind off centre 12 (14, 16) sts, knit to end.

Cont on last 16 (17, 19) sts. Dec 1 st at neck edge on foll 2nd row once, then on every foll 4th row 1 (2, 3) times more, then on every foll 2nd row until 2 sts rem. Work 2 sts tog, fasten off.

Ret to rem sts, rejoin B at neck edge and finish to match other side.

Trim for sides

With RS facing, 3.25 mm (No. 10) needles and B, evenly pick up 44 (48, 54) sts along side edge of Collar. Knit 1 row, inc 1 st at each end of row. Cont in g st by knitting every row in stripes of 4 rows A and 4 rows B AT SAME TIME inc 1 st on every row at pointed end and inc 1 st every 2nd row at other end 4 times. Cast/bind off in B on next row.

Trim for lower edge

With RS facing, 3.25 mm (No. 10) needles and B, pick up 1 st in each of cast-on sts AT SAME TIME inc 4 sts evenly across row. 48 (52, 58) sts. Knit 1 row and inc 1 st each end of the row. Cont in g st in stripes of 4 rows A and 4 rows B AT SAME TIME inc 1 st each end of every 2nd row 4 times more. Cast/bind off in B on next row. Join Trims to form corners.

BOW TIE

With 4.00 mm (No. 8) needles and C, cast on 11 sts. Work in K1, P1 rib for 8 rows.

Next row: K1, (K2 tog) 5 times.

Beg with purl row work 3 rows st st.

Next row: K1, (K1 in front and back lp of next st) 5 times. 11 sts.

Cont in P1, K1 rib for 8 rows. Cast/bind off in rib.

With 3.25 mm (No. 10) needles and C, cast on 5 sts. Work in K1, P1 rib for 5 cm (2 in). Cast/bind off in rib. Place this piece at centre of other piece and sew to form a Bow Tie.

LONG TIE

With 4.00 mm (No. 8) needles and C, cast on 9 sts. Work in K1, P1 rib until 10 cm (4 in), ending with WS row.

Next row: K1, K2 tog, P1, K1, P1, sl1, K1, psso, K1.

Next row: P2, K1, P1, K1, P2.

Next row: K1, P2 tog, K1, P2 tog, K1. 5 sts.

Cont in P1, K1 rib until 18 cm (7 in) from beg, ending with WS row.

Next row: K1, (K1 in front and back loop

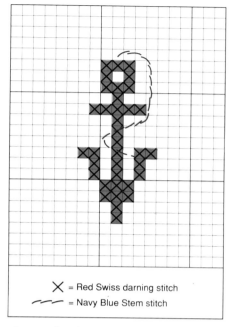

X = Red Swiss darning stitch
⌒ = Navy Blue Stem stitch

of next st) 4 times. 9 sts.

Cont in P1, K1 rib for further 8 cm (3¼ in). Cast/bind off in rib.

With 3.25 mm (No. 10) needles and C, cast on 5 sts. Work in st st for 10 cm (4 in). Cast/bind off. This is the attachment piece. Tie the Long Tie to attachment piece with a slip knot.

TO MAKE UP

Lightly press on wrong sides. Sew shoulder, side and sleeve seams. Set Sleeves into armholes. Leaving B stripe sections free, attach Collar in place, then sew B sections tog at centre front to form point of Collar. Sew top edges of side vent Trims in place. Stitch motif onto left front from Graph, using Swiss darning or knitting stitch. Attach Bow or Long Tie at V point.

CROCHET SKIRT

NOTE: To change colour in tr fabric: work in tr until 1 st rem before next colour, *then work 1 tr into next st as follows: yoh, insert hook in next st, yoh and draw through, yoh and draw through 2 loops on hook, drop colour and keep it at wrong side of piece, pick up next colour, yoh and draw through last 2 loops on hook, then cont to work with new colour until 1 tr rem before change of colour, rep from * to change colour.

BACK AND FRONT ALIKE

With 4.00 mm (No. 8) hook and B, make 18 (19, 22) ch, with A make 18 ch (all sizes), with B 20 (22, 22) ch, with A 18 ch,

with B 20 (21, 24) ch.

1st row: (WS) with B make 1 tr in 4th ch from hook, 1 tr in each of next 16 (17, 20) ch, with A 1 tr in each of next 18 ch, with B 1 tr in each of next 20 (22, 22) ch, with A 1 tr in each of next 18 ch, with B 1 tr in each of last 18 (19, 22) ch. 92 (96, 102) tr, counting 3 ch as 1 tr.

2nd row: With B (1 dc, 2 ch) in 1st tr, 1 tr in each of next 16 (17, 20) tr, *with B, 1 trF, with A 1 tr in each of next 4 tr, 1 trB, 1 tr in each of next 8 tr, 1 trB, 1 tr in each of next 4 tr, with B 1 trF *, with B 1 tr in each of next 18 (20, 20) tr, rep from * to * once, with B 1 tr in each of next 17 (18, 21) tr.

3rd row: With B (1 dc, 2 ch) in 1st tr, 1 tr in each of next 16 (17, 20) tr, *with B 1 trB, with A 1 tr in each of next 4 tr, 1 trF, 1 tr in each of next 8 tr, 1 trF, 1 tr in each of next 4 tr, with B 1 trB *, with B 1 tr in each of next 18 (20, 20) tr, rep from * to * once, with B 1 tr in each of last 17 (18, 21) tr.

Rep 2nd and 3rd rows for patt. Cont in patt until work meas 15 (20½, 23) cm [6 (8, 9) in] from beg or length req, ending with WS row. Fold work at each trF to make two inverted pleats. Using B only cont as follows:

Next row: (1 dc, 2 ch) in 1st tr, 1 tr in each

of next 12 (13, 16) tr, *miss 1 trB, working through all thicknesses 1 tr in each of next 4 tr, inserting hook behind next 2 trFS work 1 trF, working through all thicknesses 1 tr in each of next 4 tr, miss 1 trB*, 1 tr in each of next 10 (12, 12) tr, rep from * to * once, 1 tr in each of last 13 (14, 17) tr. 54 (58, 64) tr rem.

Next row: (1 dc, 2 ch) in 1st tr, 1 tr in each tr to end.

Work 0 (0, 1) row of tr.

Next row: (1 dc, 2 ch) in 1st tr, dec 1 tr, 1 tr in each of next 14 (15, 17) tr, dec 1 tr, 1 tr in each of next 16 (18, 20) tr dec 1 tr, 1 tr in each of next 14 (15, 17) tr, dec 1 tr, 1 tr in last tr.

Next row: (1 dc, 2 ch) in 1st tr, 1 tr in each tr to end.

Next row: (1 dc, 2 ch) in 1st tr, dec 1 tr, 1 tr in each of next 13 (14, 16) tr, dec 1 tr, 1 tr in each of next 14 (16, 18) tr, dec 1 tr, 1 tr in each of next 13 (14, 16) tr, dec 1 tr, 1 tr in last tr, fasten off.

WAISTBAND
Lightly press on wrong side. Sew up side seams. With RS facing and 4.00 mm (No. 8) hook, rejoin B at side seam, 1 ch, 1 dc in each tr around top edge, sl st to 1st dc, TURN.

Next 2 rnds: 3 ch, 1 tr in each st to end, sl st to top of 3 ch, TURN.

Next rnd: (WS) 3 ch, * 1 ch, miss 1 tr, 1 trF, rep from * to last tr, 1 ch, miss 1 tr, sl st to

3rd of 4 ch, TURN.

Next rnd: 4 ch, * 1 tr in next tr, 1 ch, rep from * to end, sl st to 3rd of 4 ch, fasten off.

STRAPS
Make 2
With 4.00 mm (No. 8) hook and B, make 5 ch, (1 dc, 2 ch) in 2nd ch from hook, 1 tr in each of next 3 ch. 4 tr. Cont in tr until piece meas 33 (41, 48) cm [11 (16, 19) in] or length req, then cont for Trim as follows: Change to 3.00 mm (No. 11) hook, 1 ch, * work 2 dc loosely along side of tr, 2 ch, sl st to top of last dc, rep from * along 3 sides, leave one short edge, fasten off - this is the back end.

TO FINISH OFF
Cut elastic to waist size and join ends to form a circle. Place elastic inside Waistband. Fold 2 rnds of Waistband to inside over elastic and stitch loosely.

At top edge of Waistband above pleat, make 3 ch, miss 2 sts, sl st to next st, TURN, 1 ch, work 5 dc in ch loop, sl st to next st on Waistband, fasten off. Make another button loop to match.

Attach Straps to inside Waistband at back. Sew button on end of each Strap.

PANTS
RIGHT LEG
With 3.25 mm (No. 10) needles and B, cast on 60 (66, 72) sts. Work 8 rows st st. Purl 1 row for hemline. Change to 4.00 mm (No. 8) needles, and beg with purl row cont in st st*. Work 9 rows, ending with WS row.

Shape back
Next 2 rows: K7 (8, 9) sts, TURN, sl1, purl to end.

Next 2 rows: K14 (16, 18) sts, TURN sl1, purl to end.

Cont to shape in this way working 7 (8, 9) sts more each time until 28 (32, 36) sts have been worked, TURN, sl1, purl to end. Cont to work front crease as follows:

1st row: K45 (49, 53) sts, sl1 knitwise, K14 (16, 18) sts.

2nd row: P14 (16, 18) sts, yrn, P1 for front crease, P45 (49, 53) sts.

3rd row: K45 (49, 53) sts, sl1 knitwise, then drop next loop made by yrn for front crease, K14 (16, 18) sts.

Rep last 2 rows for front crease. **Cont in this way until work meas 11 (12, 13) cm [4 1/2 (4 3/4, 5) in] from hemline at front edge, ending with WS row.

Shape crotch
Working front crease as before inc 1 st

each end of next row, then on every foll 6th row twice more, then on foll 4th row once, then on every foll 2nd row 3 times. 74 (80, 86) sts. Work 1 row **.

Cast on 3 (4, 5) sts at beg of next row for Back, then 3 sts (all sizes) at beg of next row for Front 80 (87, 94) sts. ***Place marker at centre of last row.

Shape leg
Working front crease as before, dec 1 st at each end of next row, then on every foll 2nd row 3 times more, then on every foll 4th row twice, then on every foll 6th row twice, then on foll 8th row once. 62 (69, 76) sts rem.

Cont straight on these rem sts until work meas 25 (29, 37) cm [9 3/4 (11 1/2, 14 1/2) in] or length req from last marker for Leg, ending with WS row. Change to 3.25 mm (No. 10) needles and knit 12 rows. Cast/ bind off.

LEFT LEG
Work as for Right Leg to *, then work 8 rows in st st, ending with RS row.

Shape back
Next 2 rows: P7 (8, 9) sts, TURN, sl1, knit to end.

Next 2 rows: P14 (16, 18) sts, sl1, knit to end.

Cont to shape in this way working 7 (8, 9) sts more each time until 28 (32, 36) sts have been worked, TURN, sl1, knit to end, then purl 1 row over all sts.

Cont to work front crease as follows:
1st row: K14 (16, 18) sts, sl1 knitwise, K45 (49, 53) sts.

2nd row: P45 (49, 53) sts, yrn, P1 for front crease, P14 (16, 18) sts.

3rd row: K14 (16, 18) sts, sl1 knitwise, then drop next loop made by yrn – for front crease, K45 (49, 53) sts.

Rep last 2 rows for front crease and work from ** to ** of Right Leg.
Working front crease as before
Shape crotch
Cast on 3 sts (all sizes) at beg of next row for Front, then 3 (4, 5) sts at beg of next row for Back. 80 (87, 94) sts. Work as for Right Leg from *** to end.

TO MAKE UP
Lightly press on wrong side. Press creases. Sew up centre back and front seams, then inside leg seams. Cut elastic to waist size and join ends tog to form circle. Place it inside hem, catching sts loosely to keep hem in place.

FINGER PUPPETS

FATHER

With blue, cast on 21 sts.

1st row: K1, (P1, K1) 10 times. Rep 1st row 5 times more. Work 6 rows st st. Change to gold and work 8 rows st st. Change to sandy brown, work 5 rows st st.

Next row: P5, *(P1 in front loop, yrn, P1 in back loop) in next st for ear, TURN, K3, TURN, P3, slip 1st 2 sts over st just worked *, P9, rep from * to * once, P5.

Work 6 rows more in st st then on next row work K1, (K2 tog) 10 times. Purl 1 row on rem 11 sts. Break off yarn, leaving a length of yarn attached. Thread end of yarn through rem sts and draw up tightly. Secure sts, then cont to sew seam.

MOTHER

With red, cast on 40 sts. Knit 1 row.

2nd row: Work (K2 tog) to end.

Knit 1 row on rem 20 sts, then work in K1, P1 rib for 15 rows.

Change to natural and work 12 rows st st. On next row work (K2 tog) 10 times. Purl 1 row on rem 10 sts.

Break off, leaving length of yarn attached. Thread end of yarn through rem sts and draw up tightly. Secure sts, then cont to sew seam.

GRANDFATHER

With grey, cast on 21 sts.

1st row: K1, (P1, K1) 10 times. Rep 1st row 5 times more. Work 10 rows st st. On

MATERIALS

Yarn: 5 ply pure wool crepe:

For father: Small quantity each of blue, gold, sandy brown, caramel, dark brown and red; 17 cm (6³/₄ in) narrow ribbon

For mother: Small quantity each of red, natural, yellow, and navy; small doll's hat

For grandfather: Small quantity each of grey, sandy brown, white, blue and mauve; 17 cm (6³/₄ in) narrow ribbon

For sister: Small quantities each of hot pink, emerald, light pink, dark brown and red

For baby: Small quantities each of royal blue, light pink, gold and red; 20 cm (8 in) narrow lace

Notions: For all puppets: One pair of 3.25 (3¹/₄) mm (No. 10) needles; clear-drying craft glue; wool sewing needle

MEASUREMENTS

Adults: 8.5 cm (3³/₈ in) high
Sister: 7 cm (2³/₄ in) high
Baby: 6 cm (2³/₈ in) high

next row work K1, (yfwd, K2 tog) 10 times. Purl 1 row. Change to sandy brown and work 5 rows st st.

Next row: P5, *(P1 in front loop, yrn, P1 in back loop) of next st for ear, TURN, K3, TURN, P3, slip 1st 2 sts over st just worked *, P9, rep from * to * once, P5.

Work 6 rows more st st. Next row work K1, (K2 tog) 10 times. Purl 1 row on rem 11 sts. Break off, leaving a length of yarn at-

tached. Thread end of yarn through rem sts and draw up tightly. Secure sts then cont to sew seam.

SISTER

With hot pink, cast on 20 sts. Knit 2 rows. With emerald, knit 2 rows. Change to hot pink and work in K1, P1 rib for 10 rows. Change to light pink and work 10 rows st st. On next row work (K2 tog) 10 times. Purl 1 row on rem 10 sts.

Break off, leaving a length of yarn attached. Thread end of yarn through rem sts and draw up tightly. Secure sts, then cont to sew seam.

BABY

With royal blue, cast on 20 sts. Work in K1, P1 for 3 cm (1¹/₄ in). Change to light pink and work 10 rows st st.

On next row work (K2 tog) 10 times. Purl 1 row on rem 10 sts.

Break off, leaving a length of yarn attached. Thread end of yarn through rem sts and draw up tightly. Secure sts then cont to sew seam.

TO MAKE UP

Father: Stitch eyes with dark brown and mouth with red. Fray or untwist length of caramel yarn. Wind it round 3 fingers and tie firmly at centre, then cut through looped ends. Attach to top of head, by sewing or glueing. Thread narrow ribbon between sts around top row of gold and tie.

Mother: Stitch eyes with navy and mouth with red. Fray length of yellow yarn. Wind it round 4 fingers and tie firmly at centre, then cut through looped ends. Attach to top of head with sewing or glueing. Trim hair in style. Glue hat over hair.

Grandfather: Stitch eyes with blue and mouth with mauve. With white, stitch loops round back of head, beg and ending above ears. Thread narrow ribbon through holes and tie at centre front.

Sister: Stitch eyes with dark brown and mouth with red. Wind dark brown around 4 fingers and tie firmly at centre, then cut through looped ends. Attach to top of head with sewing or glueing and trim to style.

Baby: Stitch eyes with royal blue and mouth with red. Fray length of gold yarn. Wind it around 2 fingers and tie firmly at centre. Cut through looped ends. Attach to top of head with sewing or glueing. Making pin-tucks, sew lace around body at change of colours.

Growing Up

Plant a seed on the back of this lovely jumper, add a little water and a lot of loving care and watch it grow into a into a wonderful, spreading tree on the front! Even the sleeves have pictures from this magical garden.

TREE JUMPER

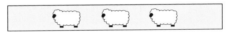

BACK
With 3.00 mm (No. 11) needles and Lb, cast on 93 (101) sts. Work in K1, P1 rib for 5 cm (2 in) ending with WS row. Change to 3.75 mm (No. 9) needles and st st *.
Work from Graph 1 until 114 (130) rows have been worked.

Shape shoulders
Still working from Graph, cast/bind off 7 (8) sts at beg of next 2 rows. 79 (85) sts.
Next row: Cast/bind off 8 (8) sts, knit until 19 (21) sts on right needle, TURN.
Cont on these 19 (21) sts. Dec 1 st at neck edge on next 3 rows AT SAME TIME cast/bind off at beg of every 2nd row 8 (9) sts twice.
Ret to rem sts, slip centre 25 (27) sts on st holder, rejoin yarn at neck edge and complete to match other side.

FRONT
Work as Back to *.
Work from Graph 2 until 96 (110) rows have been worked. Cont to work from Graph 2.

Shape neck
Next row: K39 (42) sts, TURN.
Cont on these 39 (42) sts and cast/bind off at neck edge on next and every foll 2nd row 2 sts 3 times, 1 st twice. 31 (34) sts.
Cont on these rem sts working from Graph

2 until 114 (130) rows have been worked.
Shape shoulder
Cast/bind off at beg of next and every foll 2nd row 7 (8) sts once, 8 (8) sts once, 8 (9) sts twice.
Ret to rem sts, slip centre 15 (17) sts onto st holder, rejoin yarn at neck edge and complete to match other side.
SLEEVES
With 3.00 mm (No. 11) needles and Lb, cast on 43 (45) sts. Work in K1, P1 rib for 4 cm (1¹/₂ in) ending with RS row.
Inc row: Rib 6 (7) sts, (inc 1 st in next st, rib 5 sts) rep ending with rib 6 (7) sts instead of 5 sts. 49 (51) sts.
Change to 3.75 mm (No. 9) needles and st st.

MATERIALS
Yarn: 5 ply pure wool 50 g (2 oz) balls: 1 (1) ball light brown (Lb); 3 balls sky blue (Sb); 8 m skeins of tapestry wool: 6 skeins green (G); 6 skeins dark green (Dg); 1 skein black (Bk); 3 skeins lilac (L); 2 skeins yellow (Y); 2 skeins red (R); 2 skeins brown (Br); 5 skeins dark brown (Dbr); 1 skein blue (B); 3 skeins white (W); 2 skeins beige (Bg); 1 skein light orange (Lo); 1 skein pink (P); 1 skein emerald green (Eg)
Notions: One pair each 3.75 (3³/₄) mm (No. 9) and 3.00 (3) mm (No. 11) knitting needles

MEASUREMENTS
To fit underarm	61 (66) cm
	24 (26) in
Garment measures	
	69 (76) cm
	27 (29) in
Length	37 (41) cm
	14¹/₂ (16) in
Sleeve seam	26 (31) cm
	10 (12) in

TENSION
26 sts and 36 rows to 10 cm (4 in) over picture knit in st st, using 3.75 mm (No. 9) needles.
It is important to knit a tension square and to work to the stated tension in order to obtain the required measurements. If your square is bigger use finer needles. If your square is smaller use thicker needles.

Work from Graph 3 for Left Sleeve and from Graph 4 for Right Sleeve AT SAME TIME inc 1 st each end of 5th row, then on every foll 4th row 5(4) times more, then on every foll 6th row 7 (10) times. 75 (81) sts.
Cont straight on these sts until 78 (96) rows have been worked. Cast/bind off loosely.

TO MAKE UP
Sew in all ends. Lightly press on wrong side. Sew right shoulder seam.

NECKBAND
With RS facing and 3.00 mm (No. 11) needles, matching colours, pick up and knit 22 (23) sts on left side of front neck, knit up sts from st holder, evenly inc 3 sts at centre front neck, knit 22 (23) sts on right side of front neck, 4 sts (both sizes) on right side of back neck, knit up sts from st holder and evenly inc 4 sts at centre back neck, knit 4 sts on left side of back neck. 99 (105) sts. Work in K1, P1 rib for 6 cm (2¹/₂ in). Loosely cast/bind off in rib.

TO FINISH OFF
Sew left shoulder seam. Using Stem stitch and Y, embroider rays around sun, detail of apron bow and water from the watering can as marked on Graph. Fold Neckband in half to inside and loosely slipstitch in place. Place centre of Sleeves to shoulder seams and sew Sleeves in place. Sew up side and sleeve seams.

KEY		----- Stem stitch	
▨	Lb	▨	Br
☐	Sb	▨	Dbr
☐	G	▨	B
▨	Dg	☐	W
■	Bk	☐	Bg
▨	L	☐	Lo
☐	Y	▨	P
▨	R	▨	Eg

Graph 1

Back

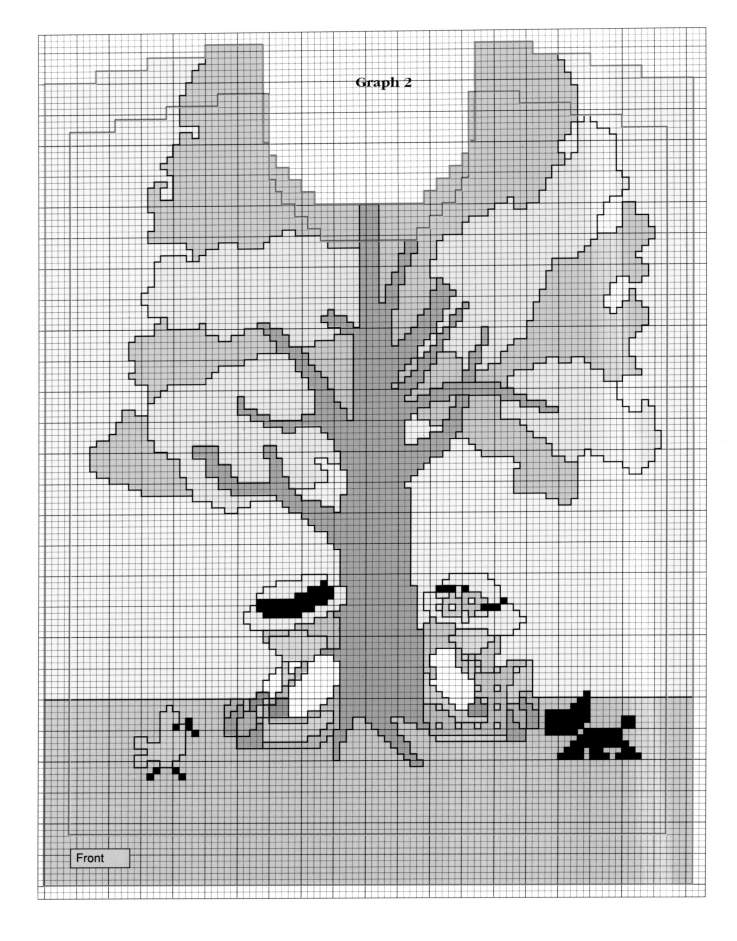

Graph 2

Front

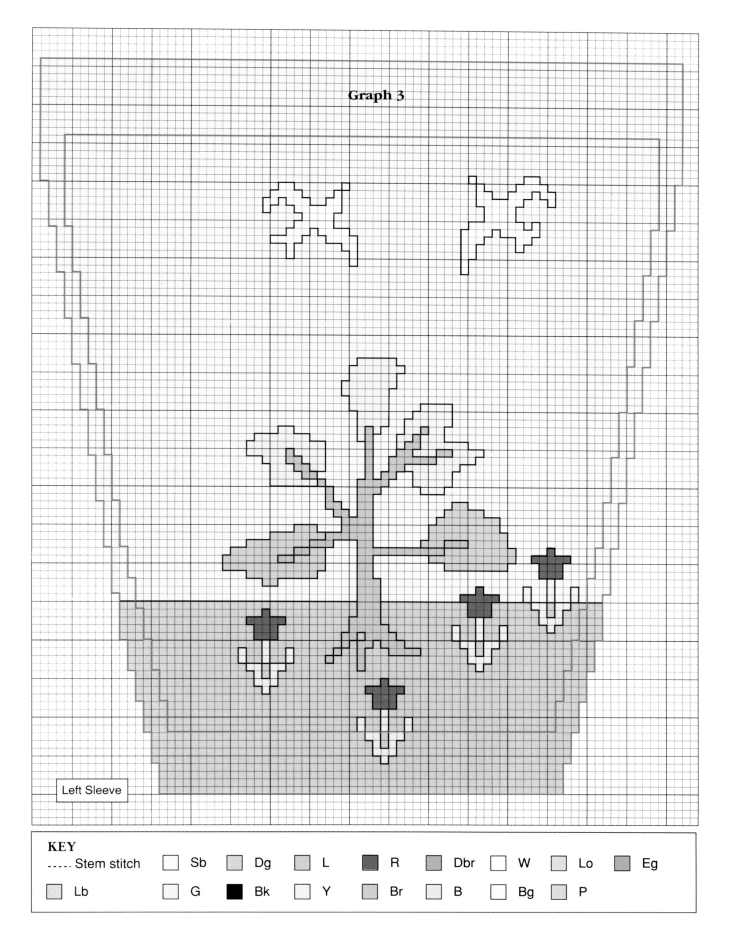

Graph 3

Left Sleeve

KEY

---- Stem stitch　Sb　Dg　L　R　Dbr　W　Lo　Eg

Lb　G　Bk　Y　Br　B　Bg　P

19

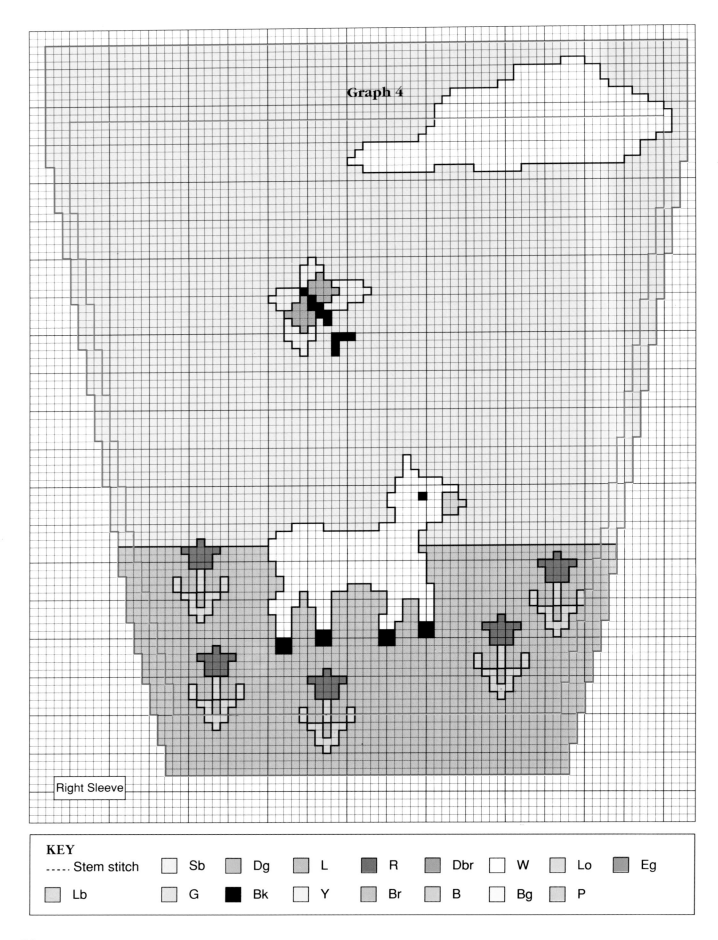

Graph 4

Right Sleeve

KEY

- - - - Stem stitch | Sb | Dg | L | R | Dbr | W | Lo | Eg

Lb | G | Bk | Y | Br | B | Bg | P

20

CHAUNCEY CHIMP

MATERIALS
Yarn: 8 ply pure new wool 50 g (2oz) balls: 1¹/₂ balls Main Colour (MC); 1 ball Contrast Colour (A)
Notions: Set of four 3.25 (3¹/₄) mm (No. 10) knitting needles; 2 buttons for eyes and 2 buttons for fastening arms; polyester fibre for filling

MEASUREMENT
Approx 38 cm (15 in) high

SPECIAL ABBREVIATION
M1 = Make 1 st: Insert right hand needle point from back of work and under horizontal loop before next st, lift it up, then insert left hand needle point in front loop and knit from this position

NOTE
Feet, legs, body and head are worked in one piece

FIRST FOOT AND LEG
With 2 needles and MC, cast on 44 sts. Work in st st. Work 4 rows.
Shape foot
1st row: K20, K2 tog tbl, TURN.
* **2nd row:** Sl1, P9, P2 tog, TURN.
3rd row: Sl1, K9, K2 tog tbl, TURN.
Rep last 2 rows 5 times, then 2nd row once more. 30 sts rem. Break off yarn, TURN, slip all sts onto left hand needle. With RS facing, join MC to first st and work over all sts for 40 rows. Cast/bind off 6 sts at beg of next 2 rows. 18 sts rem*. Break off yarn. Leave sts on needle.
SECOND FOOT AND LEG
Work as First Foot and Leg until 4 rows of st st from beg have been worked.
Shape foot
1st row: K33, K2 tog tbl, TURN.
Work as for First Foot from * to *. Do not break off yarn. Leave work aside.
CROTCH
With 2 needles and MC, cast on 6 sts and work 12 rows in st st. Break off yarn. With RS facing, slip these 6 sts onto end of 2nd Leg, then return to beg of 2nd Leg, and

cont for Body as follows:
1st rnd: With 1st needle K13, with 2nd needle K5, then K6 over Crotch, and K5 from other Leg, with 3rd needle K13, pick up 6 sts along RS of cast-on edge of Crotch. 48 sts.
Slip last 3 sts onto 4th needle. First of these 4 sts is beg of rnd and is centre back. First 3 sts for next rnd are already worked. Cont in rnds of st st by knitting every rnd. Work 2 rnds.
Next rnd: K2, (M1, K4) rep to last 2 sts, M1, K2. 60 sts.
Work 2 rnds straight.
Shape back-opening and work in colours for Front as follows:
1st row: With MC inc 1 st in first st, K26, with A K6, with MC from separate ball K26,

inc 1 st in last st, TURN. 62 sts.
2nd row: P27 MC, P8 A, P27 MC, TURN.
3rd row: K26 MC, K10 A, K26 MC, TURN.
4th row: P25 MC, P12 A, P25 MC, TURN.
5th row: K24 MC, K14 A, K24 MC, TURN.
6th, 8th rows: Using same colours as on needle, purl to end, TURN.
7th, 9th rows: Knit 1 st less in MC at beg and end of rnd, and 2 sts more in A at centre, TURN.
10th row: As 6th row.
11th row: With MC, K22, with A K18, with MC K22, TURN.
Rep last 2 rows 5 times, then 6th row once more.
Next row: With MC, knit until the first st of A is worked in MC, with A knit to 1 st before next MC, with MC knit to end, TURN.

Next row: Using same colours as on needle purl to end, TURN.

Rep last 2 rows 3 times, then cont to work 1 st more in MC at beg and end of rnd, and 2 sts less in A at centre ON EVERY ROW 4 times.

Next row: With MC K2 tog, knit to last 2 sts, sl1, K1, psso. 60 sts. Cont in rnds of st st in MC only as follows:

Shape neck

Dec 10 sts evenly on next and every foll 3rd rnd until 30 sts rem, then work 2 rnds straight.

Next rnd: (K1 tbl) rep to end.

Cont for Head as follows:

Evenly inc 15 sts on every 3rd rnd twice. 60 sts. Work 27 rnds straight then evenly dec 10 sts on next and every foll 2nd rnd until 10 sts rem. Work 1 rnd on rem 10 sts. Break off, leaving a length of yarn. Thread end of yarn through rem sts, draw up tightly and securely fasten off.

HANDS AND ARMS

With 2 needles and A, cast on 2 sts. Work in st st, inc 1 st each end of 1st and 3rd rows, then work 3 rows straight*. Break off yarn. Leave work aside. Make another piece the same to *, and cont as follows:

Next row: Cast on 3 sts and knit all sts, then K6 over other piece.

Next row: Cast on 3 sts, purl all sts. 18 sts. Change to MC only.

Next row: Sl1, K1, psso, K6, M1, K2, M1, K6, K2 tog.

Next row: Purl.

Rep last 2 rows twice, then work 2 rows straight. Inc 1 st each end of next row. 20 sts. Work 11 rows straight.

Next row: K1, M1, K7, K2 tog, sl1, K1, psso, K7, M1, K1.

Work 3 rows straight. Rep last 4 rows twice.

Shape top

1st row: (Sl1, K1, psso, K6, K2 tog) twice.

2nd, 4th, 6th rows: Purl.

3rd row: (Sl1, K1, psso, K4, K2 tog) twice.

5th row: (Sl1, K1, psso, K2, K2 tog) twice.

Cast/bind off. Make another one the same.

SOLES

Make 2

With 2 needles and A, cast on 5 sts. Work in st st inc 1 st each end of 1st and 3rd rows, then on every foll 8th row twice. 13 sts. Work 3 rows straight, then dec 1 st each end of next row and foll 2nd row once more.

Next row: (Toe end), P2 tog, cast/bind off to last 2 sts, P2 tog and cast/bind off.

FIRST AID

Dealing with dropped stitches is quite a simple matter if you have a crochet hook handy. Using the hook you can knit or purl each stitch up the ladder until you reach the row on the needle. It is important to purl the purl stitches and knit the knit stitches to keep your pattern correct. Using this same method you can quite easily correct a wrong stitch, even one some rows down. Drop the stitch immediately above the mistake, forming a ladder down to it. Use the crochet hook method to pick up all the stitches back up to the needle, correcting the mistake as you go. Picking up dropped stitches is always easier with a thinner needle.

MUZZLE

With 4 needles and A, cast on 48 sts and join in circle. Place marker in first st to denote beg of rnd. Knit 1 rnd.

Shape chin

Working in rows cont as follows:

1st row: K22 on 1 needle, TURN, leave rem 26 sts on 2 needles for upper section.

2nd row: Sl1, P19, TURN.

3rd row: Sl1, K17, TURN.

4th row: Sl1, P15, TURN.

Cont in this way, working 2 sts less each time until row of Sl1, P7 has been worked, TURN, sl1, knit to st above marker to complete rnd, knit 1 rnd over all sts.

Keeping st above marker at beg of 1st needle, rearrange sts evenly on 3 needles and cont in rnds of st st.

Next rnd: (Sl1, K1, psso, K20, K2 tog) twice.

Next rnd: Knit.

Next rnd: (Sl1, K1, psso, K18, K2 tog) twice. 40 sts .

Working to and fro cont as follows:

Next row: K18, TURN, leave rem 22 sts on two needles.

Next row: Sl1, P15, TURN.

Next row: Sl1, K13, TURN.

Next row: Sl1, P11, TURN.

Cont in this way working 2 sts less each

---

time until row of Sl1, P7 has been worked, TURN, then work sl1 and knit to stitch above marker to complete rnd. Rearrange sts onto 3 needles as before and cont in rnds as follows:

Next rnd: (Sl1, K1, psso, K16, K2 tog) twice.

Next rnd: Knit.

Next rnd: (Sl1, K1, psso, K14, K2 tog) twice. 32 sts rem.

Next rnd: Knit.

Cast/bind off. Fold cast/bind off edge flat and sew across through all thicknesses for Mouth. Cont for Face as follows:

With RS row facing, two needles and A, pick up and knit 1 st in each of centre 16 sts along upper section for Muzzle and work in st st as follows:

1st, 3rd, 5th rows: Purl.

2nd row: (K1, M1, K6, M1, K1) twice.

4th row: (K1, M1, K8, M1, K1) twice.

6th row: (K1, M1, K10, M1, K1) twice. 28 sts.

Work 5 rows straight ending with WS row.

Next row: K14, TURN.

** Cont on these 14 sts and dec 1 st each end of next 3 rows.

Next row: K2 tog, cast/bind off to last 2 sts, K2 tog, cast/bind off. Ret to rem 14 sts, rejoin A at centre, knit 1 row, then work as other side from ** to end.

EARS

Make 2 each in MC and A

With 2 needles, cast on 11 sts. Work in st st and inc 1 st each end of 3rd and 5th rows. 15 sts.

Work 7 rows straight, then dec 1 st each end of next 2 rows, then decreasing 1 st at each end cast/bind off.

With right sides tog sew MC and A pieces tog, leaving cast-on edge open. Turn right side out.

TO MAKE UP

Sew inside leg seams. Join cast/bind off edge of legs to each side of Crotch. Sew Soles into place. Fill firmly, distributing filling with needle point for better shaping. Close opening, leaving 3 cm (1$\frac{1}{4}$ in) open around top edge of Arms. Sew seam on Arms. Fill Arms. Insert button in top of each Arm to secure, then with thick cotton securely attach Arms through Body and through buttons. Close openings. Neatly sew face section onto front of Head with flat seam, then attach Muzzle section, filling when piece is half sewn. Securely attach Ears. Sew on buttons for eyes.

CROCHET BALL

MATERIALS

Yarn: 5 ply pure new crepe 50 g (2 oz) balls: $\frac{1}{2}$ ball yellow, small quantity each in 13 other colours
Notions: One 3.00 (3) mm (No. 10) crochet hook; polyester fibre for filling

MEASUREMENTS

Approx 38 cm (15 in) in circumference
Each side of motif to measure 4 cm ($1\frac{1}{2}$ in) on every side edge

MOTIF

Make 12
1st rnd: Wind yellow yarn twice around index finger of left hand for base loop,

insert hook through base loop, yon and draw a loop through, keeping base loop firmly with 2 fingers of left hand, work 3 ch, then 14 tr in base loop, draw up end of yarn tightly to close base loop, sl st to top of 3 ch. 15 tr counting 3 ch as 1 tr, fasten off.
2nd rnd: With RS facing, join a colour to top of 3 ch where sl st is worked, 3 ch, (1 tr, 1 ch, 2 tr) in same place as join, *1 tr in each of next 2 tr, (2 tr, 1 ch, 2 tr) in next tr, rep from * 3 times more, 1 tr in each of last 2 tr, sl st to top of 3 ch.
3rd rnd: 3 ch, 1 tr in next tr, *(1 tr, 1 ch, 1 tr) in next 1 ch sp, 1 tr in each of next 6 tr, rep from * 3 times more, (1 tr, 1 ch, 1 tr) in next 1 ch sp, 1 tr in each of last 4 tr, sl st to top of 3 ch, fasten off.
Always working 1st rnd with yellow cont to make 11 more motifs in different colours.

TO MAKE UP

With wrong sides tog, matching dc to dc and with last colour, join one motif to each side of a centre motif by working dc through

all thicknesses, then join adjacent motifs tog in same way to form a cup. Join 6 other motifs in same way, making second cup, then join two cups tog in zigzag, leaving one side open. Fill ball evenly and close opening.

GAUGE YOUR TENSION

Correct tension is essential for perfect fit and shape. This is especially so if changing yarn from one type or brand to another.

What is tension?

Tension, or gauge, is simply a way of measuring the tightness or looseness of your knitting. It is affected by the type and thickness of your yarn, the size of the needles, and whether your knitting will be plain or patterned. Naturally if you are using thicker yarn you will count fewer stitches to the stated length. If your tension is too loose (too few stitches to the stated length), your garment will lack shape, stretch easily and wash poorly. If your tension is too tight (too many stitches to the stated length), your knitting will feel stiff and will not be as comfortable to wear.

How to measure it?

You must ensure that you have the same number of stitches to the stated length, usually 10 cm, as given in the pattern. To measure tension, knit a tension square in your stitch pattern

and count the stitches. It is best to knit a piece bigger than 10 cm square. Cast off then press your sample lightly, if necessary. Pin out your square on a firm surface. Align the top of a ruler with a row of stitches. Place a pin at 0, and another at 10 cm. Count the stitches between the pins. To measure row tension, place the ruler vertically.

Adjusting your tension

If you have fewer stitches to 10 cm, use thinner needles. If you have more stitches to 10 cm, use thicker needles. Remember if you change yarn, needles or pattern, you must knit a new tension square.

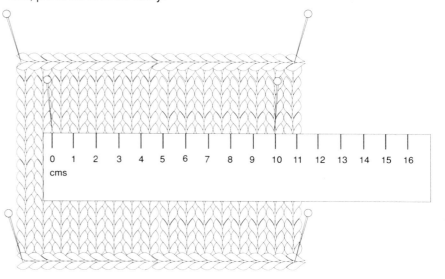

Bunny
Love

What is soft, lovable,
warm and cuddly?
Both of us are! My
granny knitted my
suit – I wonder who
made Winston's?

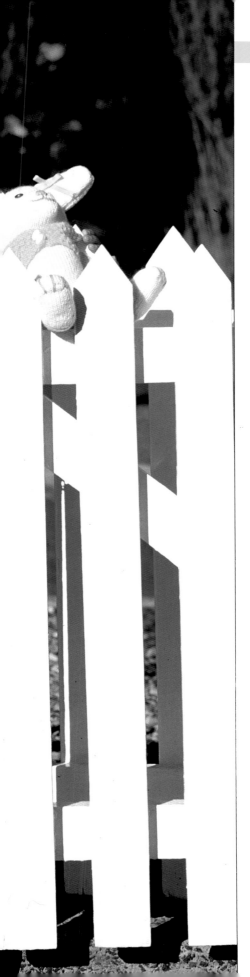

BUNNY SUIT

JUMPER
BACK
With 3.25 mm (No. 10) needles and A, cast on 67 (73, 79) sts. Work in K1, P1 rib for 4 (4, 5) cm [1^1/$_2$ (1^1/$_2$, 2) in], ending with WS row. Change to 4.00 mm (No. 8) needles and continue for lattice patt as follows:

1st row: With A, Knit.

2nd row: With A, P1 (2, 1) sts, *yrn, P4, rep from * to last 2 (3, 2) sts, yrn, P2 (3, 2) sts.

3rd row: With B, K1 (2, 1) sts, *keeping yarn at back sl1 purlwise, then drop next extra loop, K3, rep from * ending with K1 (2, 1) sts instead of K3.

4th row: With B, P1 (2, 1) sts, *sl1 purlwise, P3, rep from * ending with P1 (2, 1) sts instead of P3.

Rep last 4 rows until work meas 10 (11, 13.5) cm [4 (4^1/$_4$, 5^1/$_4$) in] from beg, ending on a 4th row of patt. Adjust length at this point, if required, ending on a 4th row of patt.

Using A only, cont in st st for 4 rows, then cont for bunny motifs as follows:

1st row: K5 (6, 5) sts A, *K2B, K1A, K3B, K1A, K2B, K3 (4, 3) A, rep from * to last 2 sts (all sizes), K2A.

Beg with 2nd row, cont to work 24 rows from Graph as set. With A only, work 2 rows st st.

Change to lattice patt as before until the work meas 27.5 (31.5, 35.5) cm [10^3/$_4$ (12^1/$_2$, 14) in] from beg or as length adjusted, ending with WS row.

Keeping lattice patt correct, cont as follows:

Shape neck
1st row: Patt 25 (27, 29) sts, cast/bind off centre 17 (19, 21) sts, patt to end.

Cont on last 25 (27, 29) sts and dec 1 st at neck edge on next 3 rows. Cast/bind off rem 22 (24, 26) sts in patt on next row.

Ret to rem 25 (27, 29) sts, rejoin yarn at neck edge and complete to match other side.

NECKBAND
With RS facing, 3.25 mm (No. 10) needles and A, evenly pick up and knit 29 (31, 33) sts on neck edge. Work in K1, P1 rib for 7 rows. Cast/bind off in rib.

MATERIALS
Yarn:

For Jumper: 8 ply pure wool 50 g (2 oz) balls: 3 (3^1/$_2$, 4) balls yellow (A) and 1 ball (all sizes) white (B)

For Pants: 4 (4^1/$_2$, 5) balls yellow

Notions: One pair each 4.00 (4) mm (No. 8) and 3.25 (3^1/$_4$) mm (No. 10) knitting needles; 6 buttons for Jumper; 2 cm (^{3}/$_4$ in) wide elastic for Pants

MEASUREMENTS
To fit underarm

51 (56, 61) cm
20 (22, 24) in

Garment measures

56 (61, 66) cm
22 (24, 26) in

Length of Jumper

30 (33, 37) cm
11^3/$_4$ (13, 14^1/$_2$) in

Sleeve seam   20 (23, 28) cm
8 (9, 11) in

Outside leg length

49 (54, 63) cm
19^1/$_2$ (21^1/$_4$, 24^3/$_4$) in

TENSION
23 sts and 32 rows to 10 cm (4 in) over st st, using 4.00 mm (No. 8) needles. It is important to knit a tension square and to work to the stated tension in order to obtain the required measurements. If your square is bigger use finer needles. If your square is smaller use thicker needles.

SPECIAL ABBREVIATION
yrn = take yarn over, then to front of right hand needle. An extra loop is made

SHOULDER BANDS
With RS facing, 3.25 mm (No. 10) needles and A, evenly pick up and knit 26 (28, 30) sts over patt section, 7 sts over Neckband section. 33 (35, 37) sts.

Work in K1, P1 rib for 7 rows. Cast/bind off in rib.

Work other side the same.

FRONT
Work as for Back until work meas 26 (29, 32) cm [10^1/$_4$ (11^1/$_2$, 12^1/$_2$) in] from beg, or as length adjusted, ending with WS row. Keeping lattice patt correct, continue as follows:

Shape neck

1st row: Patt 27 (29, 31) sts, cast/bind off centre 13 (15, 17) sts, patt to end.
Cont on last 27 (29, 31) sts and dec 1 st at neck edge on next 5 rows (all sizes). Cont on rem 22 (24, 26) sts until work meas same as Back without shoulder band. Cast/bind off in patt on next row. Ret to rem 27 (29, 31) sts, rejoin yarn at neck edge and complete to match other side.

NECKBAND

With RS facing, 3.25 mm (No. 10) needles and A, evenly pick up and knit 39 (41, 43) sts along neck edge. Work in K1, P1 rib for 7 rows. Cast/bind off in rib.

LEFT SHOULDER BAND

With RS facing, 3.25 mm (No. 10) needles and A, evenly pick up and knit 26 (28, 30) sts over patt section, 7 sts over Neckband. 33 (35, 37) sts. Work 3 rows in K1, P1 rib.
Next row: Rib 7 (9, 9) sts, *cast/bind off 2 sts, rib until 8 (8, 9) sts on right hand needle after cast/bind off 2 sts, rep from * once, cast/bind off 2 sts, rib to end.
Next row: Rib 4 sts, *cast on 2 sts, rib 8 (8, 9) sts, rep from * once, cast on 2 sts, rib to end.
Work 2 more rows in rib as before. Cast/bind off in rib.

RIGHT SHOULDER BAND

Work as for Left Shoulder Band reversing buttonhole positions.

SLEEVES

Place front shoulder bands over back

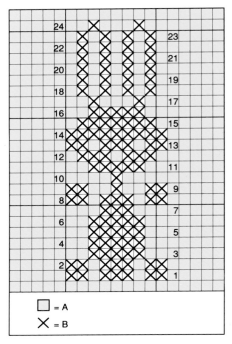

☐ = A
✕ = B

shoulder bands and catch sts together along armhole edges. Place marker at each side edge of Back and Front piece at 10 (11, 12) cm [4 (4¼, 4¾) in] below Shoulder Bands. With RS facing, 4.00 mm (No. 8) needles and A, pick up and knit 51 (55, 61) sts between markers, inserting needle through double thicknesses over shoulder bands.
Beg with purl row cont in st st. Dec 1 st each end of 14th row once, then on every foll 6th row (all sizes) until 39 (41, 43) sts rem. Cont on these stitches until sleeve meas 16 (19, 23) cm [5¼ (7½, 9) in], or length required, ending with WS row. Change to 3.25 mm (No. 10) needles and continue in K1, P1 rib for 4 (4, 5) cm [1½ (1½, 2) in]. Cast/bind off in rib.

TO MAKE UP

Sew in all ends. Press lightly on wrong side. Sew up side and sleeve seams. Sew on buttons.

PANTS

RIGHT LEG

Beg at waist, with 3.25 mm (No. 10) needles and A, cast on 66 (72, 78) sts. Work 8 rows st st. Purl 1 row for hemline. Change to 4.00 mm (No. 8) needles*. Beg with purl row work 9 rows st st, ending with WS row.

Shape back

Next 2 rows: K8 (9, 10) sts, TURN, sl1, purl to end.

Next 2 rows: K16 (18, 20) sts, TURN, purl to end.
Cont to shape in this way, working 8 (9, 10) sts more each time until 32 (36, 40) sts have been worked, TURN, sl1, purl to end.
**Cont in st st over all sts until work meas 12 (13, 14) cm [4¾ (5, 5½) in] from hemline at front edge, ending with WS row.

Shape crotch

Inc 1 st each end of next row, then on every foll 6th row twice, then foll 4th row once, then on every foll 2nd row 3 times. 80 (86, 92) sts. Work 1 row**. Cast on 4 sts (all sizes) at beg of next row, then 2 sts (all sizes) at beg of next row. 86 (92, 98) sts. ***

Place marker at centre of last row.

Shape leg

Dec 1 st each end of next row, then on every foll 2nd row 3 times more, then foll 4th row twice, then foll 6th row once, then on foll 8th row once. 70 (76, 82) sts. Cont straight on these rem sts until work meas 24 (28, 36) cm [9½ (11, 14¼) in] from marker, ending with RS row. Adjust length at this point if required, ending with RS row.

Dec row: P2 (2, 3) sts, *(P2 tog) twice, P1, rep from * to last 3 (4, 4) sts, P2 tog, P1 (2, 2) sts. 43 (47, 51) sts.
Change to 3.25 mm (No. 10) needles and work in K1, P1 rib for 5 cm (2 in). Cast/bind off loosely in rib.

LEFT LEG

Work as Right Leg to *, then beg with purl row work 8 rows st st, ending with RS row.

Shape back

Next 2 rows: P8 (9, 10) sts, TURN, sl1, knit to end.

Next 2 rows: P16 (18, 20) sts, TURN, sl1, knit to end.
Cont to shape in this way working 8 (9, 10) sts more each time until 32 (36, 40) sts have been worked, TURN, sl1, knit to end. Beg with purl row cont in st st over all sts and work from ** to ** of Right Leg. Cast on 2 sts (all sizes) at beg of next row, then 4 sts (all sizes) at beg of next row. 86 (92, 98) sts. Work as Right Leg from *** to end.

TO MAKE UP

Lightly press on wrong side. Sew up centre Back and Front seams, then sew up inside Leg seams. Cut elastic to waist size and join ends tog to form circle, then place it inside hem. Fold hem to inside and loosely stitch down into place.

HINT

Buttonholes, lace patterns and eyelets are all made with the same basic method. At a buttonhole, for example, position the yarn over or around the right hand needle before decreasing one or two stitches, depending on the size you require. Whether you place the yarn over the needle or around it depends on where you are making the buttonhole. Between two knit stitches or a purl and a knit stitch bring the yarn over (yfwd). Between two purl or a knit and a purl stitch bring the yarn around (yrn). On the next row work stitches over the hole.

WINSTON RABBIT

FIRST FOOT AND LEG
With 2 needles and MC, cast on 46 sts. Work in st st for 4 rows.

Shape foot

1st row: K19, K2 tog tbl, TURN.

***2nd row:** Sl1 purlwise, P5, P2 tog, TURN.

3rd row: Sl1 knitwise, K5, K2 tog tbl, TURN.

Rep last 2 rows 6 times, then 2nd row once more. 30 sts.

Next row: Sl1, K to end of work.

Next row: P30.

Work 16 rows straight. Cast/bind off 6 sts at beg of next 2 rows. 18 sts *. Break off yarn.

SECOND FOOT AND LEG
Work as First Foot and Leg until 4 rows of st st from beg have been worked.

Shape foot

1st row: K32, K2 tog tbl, TURN.

Work from * to * of 1st foot, do not break off yarn. Leave work aside.

CROTCH
With 2 needles and another ball of MC, cast on 4 sts. Work in st st for 2 rows.

Next row: K1, M1, K2, M1, K1.

Cont to inc by working M1 1 st from each end on every foll 4th row until there are 10 sts, then work 3 rows more, ending with WS row. Break off yarn. Slip these 10 sts to beg of First Leg.

Ret to beg of Second Leg and cont for Body as follows:

1st rnd: With 1st needle K15, with 2nd needle K3, K10 over Crotch, K3 from First Leg, with 3rd needle K15, then pick up 4 sts along right side of cast-on edge of Crotch. 50 sts.

Slip last 2 sts onto 4th needle. First st on this needle is beg of rnd and is centre back. First 2 sts for next rnd are already worked. Cont in rnds of st st by knitting every rnd. Work 1 rnd.

Next rnd: (K3, M1) 3 times, K32, (M1, K3) 3 times. 56 sts.

Work 1 rnd.

Shape base of body

1st rnd: K14 then slip last 14 sts of 3rd needle onto other end of same needle. 28 sts on 1 needle.

Divide rem 28 sts evenly onto 2 other needles and leave for Front. Work in st st rows on these 28 sts, beg with purl row

work 11 rows for Base ending with purl row.

Shape back

1st row: K17, K2 tog, K1, TURN.

2nd row: P8, P2 tog, P1, TURN.

3rd row: K9, K2 tog, K1, TURN.

4th row: P10, P2 tog, P1, TURN.

Cont in this way working 1 st more each time until all sts are worked on one needle and 18 sts rem, ending with purl row, TURN, and K9 sts. Last of these 9 sts is end of work. Slip 28 sts for Front onto one needle. Ret to 9 sts for Back. Using another needle K9 sts for Back. First of these 9 sts is beg of work and is centre back. With same needle pick up 11 sts along side of Base, with second needle K28 for Front, with third needle pick up 11 sts along side of base, then K9 from needle. 68 sts.

There should be 20 sts each on 1st and 3rd needles, and 28 sts on 2nd needle. Always keep first st of rnds at beg of 1st needle and last st at end of 3rd needle.

Cont as follows:

1st rnd: Knit.

2nd rnd: Knit to last 4 sts of 1st needle, K2

tog, K2, K28 on 2nd needle, on 3rd needle work K2, sl1, K1, psso, and knit to end of needle.

Rep last 2 rnds 3 times. 60 sts.

Keeping first st of rnd at beg of 1st needle, rearrange sts evenly on 3 needles. Knit 1 rnd.

Shape back opening

1st row: Inc 1 st in first st, knit to last st of rnd, inc 1 st in last st, TURN.

2nd row: P62, TURN.

3rd row: K62, TURN.

Rep last 2 rows 7 times, then 2nd row once more, then knit 1 row and dec 1 st at each end of the row. 60 sts. Cont in rnds of st st as before for 4 rnds.

Shape neck

Evenly dec 10 sts on next and every foll 3rd rnd until 30 sts rem. Work 2 rnds more without dec.

Next rnd: (K1 tbl) rep to end.

Shape head

Work 2 rnds straight, then evenly inc 15 sts on next rnd, then on foll 3rd rnd once more by working M1 to inc. Keeping first st of rnd at beg of 1st needle, rearrange sts evenly onto 3 needles. Work 2 rnds straight.

Shape nose

Next rnd: With 1st needle K20, then K6 from 2nd needle and slip next 8 sts onto a piece of wool for Nose, slip rem 6 sts of 2nd needle onto beg of 3rd needle, TURN.

Next row: With 1st needle P26, with 2nd needle P26, TURN.

Using 3 needles, cont on these 52 sts in st st working to and fro for further 8 rows, ending with purl row, TURN

Shape top of head

Next rnd: With 1st needle K26, with 2nd needle K20, with 3rd needle K6 and with WS facing cast on 8 sts for top of Nose, with 4th needle K6 from 1st needle and slip these 6 sts to end of 3rd needle. 60 sts.

Next rnd: With 1st needle K20. Last of these 20 sts is end of rnd, with 2nd needle K20. First of these 20 sts is beg of rnd, with 3rd needle K20.

Work 13 rnds straight, then evenly dec 10 sts on next rnd and every foll 2nd rnd until 10 sts rem. Work 1 rnd on rem 10 sts. Break off, leaving a length of yarn. Thread end of yarn through rem 10 sts, draw up tightly and fasten off securely.

NOSE
Ret to 8 sts for Nose on piece of wool. With RS facing, join A to corner before 1st of these 8 sts, K1 in corner using 3 needles, K8 from piece of wool, K1 in next corner,

MATERIALS
Yarn: 8 ply pure wool 50 g (2 oz) balls: 1½ balls Main Colour (MC); ½ ball First Contrast (A); ½ ball Second Contrast (B); small quantity of 5 ply wool in another colour for embroidery

Notions: Set of four 3.25 (3¼) mm (No. 10) knitting needles for Rabbit; one pair of 4.00 (4) mm (No. 8) knitting needles for jacket; polyester fibre for filling; 2 buttons for eyes; 2 small buttons for jacket; 2 buttons for fastening arms; 15 cm (6 in) narrow ribbon

MEASUREMENT
Approx 34 cm (13½ in) high

SPECIAL ABBREVIATION
M1 = Make 1 stitch: insert right hand needle point from back of work and under horizontal loop before next st, lift it up, then insert left hand needle point in front loop and knit from this position

NOTE
Feet, legs, body and head are worked in one piece

pick up 8 sts along side of rows, K1 in next corner, pick up 8 sts along cast-on edge of top section, K1 in next corner, pick up 8 sts along side of rows. 36 sts.

First st of 1st needle is beg of rnd. Cont in rnds of st st for 4 rnds.

Working in rows, cont as follows:

1st row: K10 and leave these 10 sts on a piece of wool for lower section, K17, sl1, K1, psso, TURN.

2nd row: Sl1, P8, P2 tog, TURN.

3rd row: Sl1, K8, sl1, K1, psso, TURN.

Rep last 2 rows 6 times, then 2nd row once more. 10 sts rem. Graft 10 sts of lower section and top section tog to close or sew them tog with a flat seam.

RIGHT PAW AND ARM

With 2 needles and A, cast on 5 sts. Work in st st. Inc 1 st each end of 1st, 3rd and 5th rows. 11 sts. Work 5 rows straight *. Break off yarn and leave work aside. Using MC work same way to *. **With MC only cont for upper section as follows:

1st row: Sl1, K1, psso, K8, M1, K1, then cont over contrast piece K1, M1, K8, K2 tog. 22 sts.

2nd row: Purl.

3rd row: Sl1, K1, psso, K8, M1, K2, M1, K8, K2 tog.

Rep last 2 rows once, then work 6 rows straight. Inc 1 st each end of next row. 24 sts.

Work 2 rows straight, ending with purl row.

Next row: K1, M1, K9, K2 tog, sl1, K1, psso, K9, M1, K1.

Work 3 rows straight, then rep last 4 rows twice.

Shape top

1st row: (Sl1, K1, psso, K8, K2 tog) twice.

2nd, 4th and 6th rows: Purl.

3rd row: (Sl1, K1, psso, K6, K2 tog) twice.

5th row: (Sl1, K1, psso, K4, K2 tog) twice.

7th row: (Sl1, K1, psso, K2, K2 tog) twice.

Cast/bind off purlwise.

LEFT PAW AND ARM

Work as Right Paw and Arm to * but beg with MC for 1st small piece, then change to A for 2nd small piece and continue to work as for Right Paw and Arm from ** to end.

SOLES

With 2 needles and A, cast on 5 sts. Work in st st. Inc 1 st each end of 1st row, then foll 4th row once, the foll 6th row once. 11 sts. Work 9 rows straight, then dec 1 st each end of next 2 rows. Cast/bind off.

EARS

Make 2 each of MC and A

With 2 needles, cast on 15 sts. Work in st st. Dec 1 st each end of 23rd row once, then foll 4th row once, then foll 2nd row twice. 7 sts. Work 1 row.

Next row: K2 tog and cast/bind off to last 2 sts, K2 tog and cast/bind off.

JACKET

With pair of 4.00 mm (No. 8) needles and B, cast on 62 sts.

1st, 2nd rows: (K1, P1) rep to end.

3rd row: P1, K1, yfwd, K2 tog, 1st button-hole is made, (P1, K1) rep to end.

4th row: (P1, K1) rep to end.

5th to 8th rows: Rep last 4 rows once.

9th row: (K1, P1) 7 times, cast/bind off 6 sts, patt until 22 sts on right hand needle after cast/bind off, cast/bind off 6 sts, patt to end.

Cont on last 14 sts in patt as before and work straight until there are 24 rows from beg. Cast/bind off in patt.

With WS facing, rejoin B to first st of centre 22 sts and cont in patt as before until there are 24 rows from beg. Cast/bind off in patt. With WS facing, rejoin B to first st of rem 14 sts and finish off as other Front. Leaving centre 5 cm (2 in) free for neck, join shoulder seams, then turn front top corners for collar and catch sts to keep collar in place. Sew on buttons.

TO MAKE UP

Sew inside Leg seams, then sew Soles into place. Join cast/bind off edge of Legs onto each side of Crotch. Fill firmly, pushing the filling with the point of a needle for better shaping. Close back opening. Leaving 3 cm (1^1/$_4$ in) around top edge of Arms, sew outer edge of Arms. Fill Arms. Insert button in top of each Arm to secure stitches, then, with thick cotton, securely attach arms through body through buttons. Close openings. Using one piece each of MC and A sew outer edges of Ears, then attach them to Head as shown. Sew on two small buttons for eyes, then embroider nose, mouth and claws. Make a pompom for a tail. Make a small tie with ribbon and securely sew onto one Ear.

Whatever the time of the year, the intrepid adventurer longs for the great outdoors with a fishing rod in his hand and the chance of catching 'the big one'.

and About

FISHERMAN'S RIB JUMPER

MATERIALS
Yarn: 5 ply pure wool crepe 50 g (2 oz) balls: 4 (4¹/₂, 5, 5¹/₂) balls Main Colour (MC); ¹/₂ ball (all sizes) each of three Contrasting Colours (A, B, C)
Notions: One pair each 3.75 (3³/₄) mm (No. 9) and 3.00 (3) mm (No. 11) knitting needles; four 3.00 (3) mm knitting needles; 2 stitch holders

MEASUREMENTS
To fit underarm
  51 (56, 61, 66) cm
  20 (22, 24, 26) in
Garment measures
  56 (61, 66, 71) cm
  22 (24, 26, 28) in
Length 30 (33, 37 41) cm
  11¹/₄ (13, 14¹/₂, 16) in
Sleeve seam 20 (23, 28, 33) cm
  8 (9, 11, 13) in

TENSION
25 sts and 52 rows to 10 cm (4 in) over fisherman's rib, using 3.75 (3³/₄) mm (No. 9) needle.
It is important to knit a tension square and to work to the stated tension in order to obtain the required measurements. If your square is bigger use finer needles. If your square is smaller use thicker needles.

SPECIAL ABBREVIATIONS
K1B = Knit into stitch in row below

BACK
Using 3.00 mm (No. 11) needles and MC cast on 73 (79, 85, 91) sts.
1st row: K2 (P1, K1) rep to last st, K1.
2nd row: K1, (P1, K1) rep to end.
Repeat these 2 rows for 4 (4, 5, 5) cm [1¹/₂ (1¹/₂, 2, 2) in], ending with RS row.
Change to 3.75 mm (No. 9) needles and cont in fisherman's rib as follows:
1st row: (WS) sl1 knitwise, knit to end.
2nd row: Sl1 knitwise, *K1B, P1, rep from * to last 2 sts, K1B, K1.

29

Rep last 2 rows until work meas 15.5 (17.5, 20.5, 23.5) cm [6 (7, 8, 9^1/$_4$) in] from beg or length required, ending with RS row.

Working in fisherman's rib as before. Beg with WS row, work in stripes of 2 rows A, 6 rows B, 2 rows A, 6 rows C ending on RS row. Keeping fisherman's rib correct cont as follows:

Shape square armholes
Using A, cast off 10 (10, 12, 12) sts at beg of next 2 rows. Using MC only, cont straight in pattern on these rem 53 (59, 61, 67) sts until work meas 28.5 (31.5, 35.5, 39.5) cm [11^1/$_4$ (12^1/$_2$, 14, 15^1/$_2$) in] from beg or as length adjusted, ending with WS row.

Shape neck
Next row: Patt 17 (19, 19, 21) sts, TURN. **Working in patt as before dec 1 st at neck edge on next and every foll 2nd row 3 times in all. Work 2 rows more on rem 14 (16, 16, 18) sts. Loosely cast/bind off in patt.

Ret to rem sts, slip centre 19 (21, 23, 25) sts onto st holder, rejoin MC at neck edge and work 1 row. Finish to match other side from **.

FRONT
Work as for Back until Front meas 25 (28, 31, 35) cm [10 (11, 12^1/$_4$, 13^3/$_4$) in] from beg, or as length adjusted, ending with WS row. Keeping patt correct cont as follows:

Shape neck
1st row: Patt 21 (25, 25, 29) sts, TURN. ***Dec 1 st at neck edge on every 2nd row 7 (9, 9, 11) times. Cont in patt on rem 14 (16, 16, 18) sts until work meas same as Back to shoulder, ending at armhole edge. Cast/bind off loosely in patt.

Ret to rem sts, leave centre 11 (9, 11, 9) sts on a st holder. Rejoin MC at neck edge and work 1 row in patt. Finish as other side from ***.

SLEEVES
Using 3.00 mm (No. 11) needles and MC, cast on 41 (43, 45, 47) sts. Work as for Back until cuff meas 4 (4, 5, 5) cm [1^1/$_2$ (1^1/$_2$, 2, 2) in], ending on RS row. Change to 3.75 mm (No. 9) needles and cont in fisherman's rib patt AT SAME TIME inc 1st each end of every 8th (8th, 9th, 10th) row until there are 55 (61, 65, 71) sts, taking all inc sts into patt.

Cont straight in patt on these sts until sleeve meas 16.5 (19.5, 24.5, 29.5) cm [6^1/$_2$ (7^3/$_4$, 9^1/$_2$, 11^1/$_2$) in] from beg, or length required, ending with RS row. Place marker at each end of last row. Keeping fisherman's rib patt correct and beg with WS row, work in stripes of 2 (2, 8, 8) rows MC, 2 rows A, 6 rows B, 2 rows A, 6 rows C and 2 rows A. Cast off loosely in patt.

TO MAKE UP
Darn in all ends. Join shoulder seams.

NECKBAND
With RS facing, using a set of four 3.00 mm (No. 11) needles and MC, beg at left shoulder seam, pick up and knit 16 (18, 20, 22) sts on each side of front neck, 11 (9, 11, 9) sts from st holder at centre front, pick up and knit 6 sts on each side of back neck, K19 (21, 23, 25) sts from st holder at centre back. 74 (78, 86, 90) sts. Work in rnds of K1, P1 rib for 6 cm (2^1/$_2$ in). Cast/bind off loosely in rib.

TO FINISH OFF
Fold half Neckband to inside and slipstitch loosely into place. Matching centre of Sleeves to shoulder seams and placing sleeve tops above markers in square section of armhole, sew Sleeves into place. Sew up side and sleeve seams.

SWISS DARNING

Swiss darning is also known as knitting stitch or duplicate stitch. It is a simple but very effective technique for adding decoration to plain knitting without the many complications of picture knitting.

We chose Swiss darning to add the delightful motifs to our Cardigan For All Seasons.

Finish the piece of knitting to be embroidered and press and block it as instructed. Study the graph carefully before you begin. Note that one square represents one stitch and that each separate colour is indicated by its own symbol. Following the graph and taking care to use the correct colour indicated for each stitch, embroider the motif onto your knitting, using the stitching technique shown in the diagrams below. Depending on the relative thickness of the knitting yarn and the embroidery yarn, it is often a good idea to use the embroidery yarn doubled. Do not join in the embroidery yarn with knots, but darn the ends in on the wrong side.

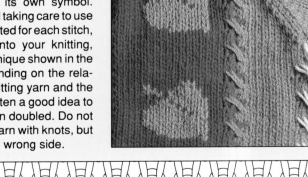

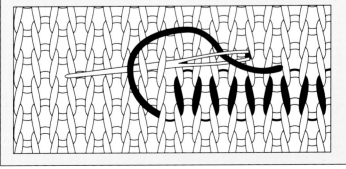

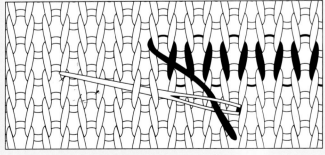

CARDIGAN FOR ALL SEASONS

Boys' and girls' Cardigan in four sizes with Swiss darned designs denoting the seasons. We've teamed each Cardigan with its own soft and cuddly toy. The Summer Ahoy Cardigan appears here; the Spring Cardigan on page 34 and the Autumn and Winter Cardigans on page 38.

BACK

With 3.00 mm (No. 11) needles and 5 separate balls, cast on 8 (10, 11, 13) sts C, 11 (11, 12, 12) sts B, 36 (40, 42, 46) sts A, 11 (11, 12, 12) sts B, 8 (10, 11, 13) sts C. 74 (82, 88, 96) sts.

Using same colours as on needle, work in K1, P1 rib for 5 cm (2 in), ending with RS row.

Change to 3.75 mm (No. 9) needles and cont for patt as follows:

1st row: (WS) *purl to 2 sts before change of colour, (yrn) twice, P2, change colour, P1, (yrn) twice, rep from * 3 times more, purl to end.

2nd row: *Knit to 4 loops before change of colour, keeping yarn at back of work sl1 purlwise, then drop 2 extra loops, K1, change colour, K1, keeping yarn at back of work sl1 purlwise, then drop 2 extra loops, rep from * 3 times more, knit to end.

3rd row: *Purl to 2 sts before change of colour, sl1 purlwise, P1, change colour, P1, sl1 purlwise, rep from * 3 times more, purl to end.

MATERIALS

Yarn: 5 ply pure wool crepe 50 g (2 oz) balls: 2 (2$^1/_2$, 3, 3$^1/_2$) balls colour A; 1(1$^1/_2$, 1$^1/_2$, 1$^1/_2$) balls colour B; 1 (1, 1, 1$^1/_2$) balls colour C. $^1/_2$ ball less each colour for a short-sleeved cardigan

Notions: One pair each 3.75 (3$^3/_4$) mm (No. 9) and 3.00 (3) mm (No. 11) knitting needles; cable needle; 6 buttons; 2 safety pins

TENSION

26$^1/_2$ sts and 36 rows to 10 cm (4 in) over st st, using 3.75 mm (No. 9) needles. It is important to knit a tension square and to work to the stated tension in order to obtain the required measurements. If your square is bigger use finer needles. If your square is smaller use thicker needles.

SPECIAL ABBREVIATIONS

yrn = yarn around needle: take yarn over, then to front of right hand needle making an extra loop

C2sl = slip next st onto cable needle and keep it in front of work, pass right hand needle point in front of next 2 sts, keeping sts on left hand needle, K1 in next sl st, then K1 into 1st missed st and drop it from left hand needle. Change colour and K1 into second missed st and drop it from left hand needle, then K1 from cable needle

MEASUREMENTS

To fit underarm

    51 (56, 61, 66) cm
    20 (22, 24, 26) in

Garment measures

    56 (61, 66, 71) cm
    22 (24, 26, 28) in

Length   30 (33, 37, 41) cm
    11$^3/_4$ (13, 14$^1/_2$, 16) in

Long sleeve seam

    20 (23, 28, 33) cm
    8 (9, 11, 13) in

Short sleeve seam

    5 (5, 5, 5) cm
    2 (2, 2, 2) in

4th row: *Knit to 2 sts before change of colour, C2sl, rep from * 3 times more, knit to end.

5th, 6th rows: Using colours as on needle purl 1 row, then knit 1 row.

Rep last 6 rows for patt.

Cont in patt until work meas 18 (21, 23, 26) cm [7 (8¼, 9, 10¼) in] from beg, ending with WS row. Adjust length at this point if required, ending on WS row.

Shape raglans

Cast/bind off 4 (5, 5, 6) sts at beg of next 2 rows.

Next row: K2 tog, patt to last 2 sts, sl1, K1, psso.

Next row: Patt without dec.

Rep last 2 rows until 26 (28, 30, 32) sts rem, ending with WS row. Cast/bind off.

LEFT FRONT

With 3.00 mm (No. 11) needles and 3 separate balls, cast on 28 (30, 32, 34) sts A, 11 (11, 12, 12) sts B, 8 (10, 11, 13) sts C. 47 (51, 55, 59) sts. Using colours as set work 4 rows in K1, P1 rib.

For boys' cardigan: Buttonhole row: Rib to last 7 sts, cast/bind off 3 sts, rib to end.

Next row: Rib and cast on 3 sts over buttonhole position.

For both boys' and girls' cardigans: Cont in rib as before until 5 cm (2 in) from beg, ending with RS row.

Next row: Rib 10 sts and leave these 10 sts on safety pin for front band. Change to 3.75 mm (No. 9) needles. *Purl to 2 sts before change of colour, (yrn) twice, P2, change colour, P1, (yrn) twice, rep from * once more, purl to end. 37 (41, 45, 49) sts.

Cont in patt as set, working C2sl on foll 3rd row, then on every foll 6th row as for Back. Work until piece meas same as for Back to raglan shaping, ending at side edge. Keeping patt correct, cont as follows:

Shape raglan

Cast/bind off 4 (5, 5, 6) sts at beg of next row. Work 1 row. Dec 1 st at raglan edge by working K2 tog on next and every foll 2nd row until 22 (23, 25, 26) sts rem, ending at front edge.

Shape neck

Cast/bind off at beg of next and every alt row 2 (3, 4, 4) sts once, 2 (2, 3, 4) sts once, 2 sts twice (all sizes), 1 st 3 times (all sizes), AT SAME TIME dec 1 st at raglan edge as before until 2 sts rem.

Work 2 sts tog, fasten off.

RIGHT FRONT

With 3.00 mm (No. 11) needles and 3 separate balls, cast on 8 (10, 11, 13) sts C, 11 (11, 12, 12) sts B, 28 (30, 32, 34) sts A. 47 (51, 55, 59) sts. Using colours as set work 4 rows in K1, P1 rib.

For girls' cardigan: Buttonhole row: Rib 4 sts, cast/bind off 3 sts, rib to end.

Next row: Rib and cast on 3 sts over buttonhole position.

For both boys' and girls' cardigans: Cont in rib as before until 5 cm (2 in) from beg, ending with RS row. Change to 3.75 mm (No. 9) needles.

Next row: *Purl to 2 sts before change of colour, (yrn) twice, P2, change colour, P1, (yrn) twice, rep from * once more, purl to last 10 sts, leave rem 10 sts on safety pin for front band. 37 (41, 45, 49) sts. Cont to work as for Left Front, reversing shapings.

LONG SLEEVES

With 3.00 mm (No. 11) needles and 5 separate balls, cast on 2 sts C (all sizes), 10 (10, 11, 11) sts B, 15 (17, 17, 19) sts A, 10 (10, 11, 11) sts B, 2 sts A (all sizes). 39 (41, 43, 45) sts.

Using colours as on needle work in K1, P1 rib for 5 cm (2 in), ending with WS row and inc 1 st in each of B sections and 4 sts in A section on last row. 45 (47, 49, 51) sts. Change to 3.75 mm (No. 9) needles and beg with 6th row cont in patt as before AT SAME TIME inc 1 st each end of 5th row once, then on every foll 6th row until there are 57 (63, 67, 73) sts, taking all inc sts into C sections.

Cont on these sts in patt without further inc until Sleeve meas 20 (23, 28, 33) cm [8 (9, 11, 13) in] from beg, ending with WS row. Adjust length at this point if required, ending with WS row. Keeping patt correct, shape raglans as for Back until 9 sts (all sizes) rem. Work 1 row. Cast/bind off.

SHORT SLEEVES

With 3.00 mm (No. 11) needles and 5 separate balls, cast on 6 (8, 9, 11) sts C, 9 (9, 10, 10) sts B, 17 (19, 19, 21) sts A, 9 (9, 10, 10) sts B, 6 (8, 9, 11) sts C. 47 (53, 57, 63) sts. Using colours as on needle work in K1, P1 rib for 7 rows. On 8th row, working in rib, inc 2 sts in each of 5 sections. 57 (63, 67, 73) sts.

Change to 3.75 mm (No. 9) needles and beg with 6th row cont in patt as before until Sleeve meas 5 cm (2 in) from beg, ending with WS row. Adjust length at this point if required, ending with WS row. Keeping patt correct, shape raglans as for Back until 9 sts (all sizes) rem. Work 1 row. Cast/bind off.

TO MAKE UP

Sew in all ends. Press lightly on wrong sides. Matching colours, sew all 4 raglan seams. Sew up side and Sleeve seams.

BAND

Transfer 10 sts from safety pin on right front for boys or on left front for girls onto 3.00 mm (No. 11) needle. Rejoin A at inner edge, inc 1 st in first st, rib to end. 11 sts. Cont in rib as before until Band, slightly stretched, fits neck edge, ending with WS row and dec 1 st at end of last row. 10 sts. Leave 10 sts on safety pin. Sew Band in place.

Mark off 6 buttonhole positions. First one is already made, 6th one will be on 4th and

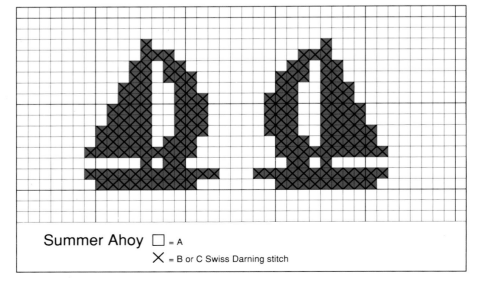

Summer Ahoy □ = A

✕ = B or C Swiss Darning stitch

5th rows of neckband, 4 others are evenly spaced between.

BUTTONHOLE BAND

Work as other Band making buttonholes as marked.

NECKBAND

With RS facing, 3.00 mm (No. 11) needles and A, K10 over right front band, pick up and knit 19 (19, 21, 21) sts on right front neck, 7 sts (all sizes) on sleeve top, 31 (33, 33, 35) sts on back neck, 7 sts (all sizes) on sleeve top, 19 (19, 21, 21) sts on left front neck, K10 over left front band. 103 (105, 109, 111) sts.

Change to B and purl 1 row. Cont in K1, P1 rib for 8 rows AT SAME TIME make a buttonhole on foll 3rd and 4th rows as before. Cast/bind off in rib.

TO FINISH OFF

Using wool sewing needle and contrast colour as illustrated, embroider motifs onto fronts from Graph as desired. Sew on buttons.

BLUEY THE BEAR

HEAD AND BODY

Worked in rnds of dc. With blue, make 4 ch, sl st to 1st ch to form circle.

1st rnd: 1 ch, 6 dc in circle, sl st to 1st dc.

2nd rnd: 1 ch, 2 dc in each of 6 dc, sl st to 1st dc.

3rd rnd: 1 ch, 1 dc in same dc as sl st, (2 dc in next dc, 1 dc in next dc) 5 times, 2 dc in last dc, do not work sl st to join rnd.

Place marker in 1st dc of last rnd to denote beg of rnd. Cont in rnd of dc in spiral, evenly inc 6 dc on every rnd taking care to inc at different position on each rnd *.

Cont to inc as given until there are 48 dc, cont to work 12 rnds of dc as before on these 48 dc. Evenly dec 6 dc on every rnd until 18 dc rem. Work 4 rnds on these 18 dc. Evenly inc 6 dc on next and every foll 2nd rnd until there are 42 dc.

Cont on these 42 dc for further 15 rnds, sl st to next dc, fasten off.

BASE

Work as for Head to *. Cont to inc as given until there are 42 dc, then work 1 rnd more without inc, sl st to next dc, fasten off.

ARMS

Make 2

MATERIALS

Yarn: 8 ply pure wool 50 g (2 oz) balls: 1¹/₂ balls blue; ¹/₂ ball natural

Notions: One 3.50 (3¹/₂) mm (No. 9) crochet hook; polyester fibre for filling; 2 flat buttons for eyes; 1 round button for nose; scrap red wool for stitching mouth; 50 cm (20 in) ribbon

MEASUREMENT

23 cm (9 in) high

Worked in rnds of dc.

With natural, make 4 ch, sl st to 1st dc to form circle, 1 ch, 6 dc in circle, sl st to 1st dc. On next rnd work 1 ch, and 2 dc in each of 6 dc. 12 dc.

Cont in rnds in spiral. Work 3 rnds, sl st to next dc, fasten off.

Join blue to a dc, and work 1 rnd, then evenly inc 4 dc on next rnd. 16 dc. Cont in rnds in spiral as before for 8 rnds, sl st to next dc, fasten off.

FOOT AND LEG

Make 2

Worked in rnds of dc. Beginning at centre of Sole, with natural, make 7 ch.

1st rnd: 1 dc in 2nd ch from hook, 1 dc in each of next 4 ch, 5 dc in last ch, working on other side of foundation ch, work 1 dc in each of next 4 ch, 4 dc in same place as 1st dc. 18 dc.

2nd rnd: 1 ch, 1 dc in each dc to end AT SAME TIME inc 3 dc around each curve, sl st to 1st dc.

3rd rnd: As 2nd rnd. 30 dc. Break off.

4th rnd: Join blue to centre dc at a curve, 1 ch, 1 dc in same place as join, 1 dc in each dc to end, sl st to 1st dc. Place marker in last dc of this rnd to denote end of rnd.

Cont in rnds of dc in spiral without sl st, and work 4 rnds.

Shape foot

1st rnd: 1 dc in each of 1st 7 dc, make 4 ch, miss next 16 dc for top of foot, 1 dc in each of last 7 dc.

2nd rnd: 1 dc in each of 1st 7 dc, 1 dc in each of next 4 ch, 1 dc in each of last 7 dc. 18 dc.

Place marker in last dc to denote end of rnd. Cont in rnds in spiral. Work 2 rnds more, evenly inc 6 dc on next rnd, then on foll 4th rnd once more. 30 dc.

Work 2 rnds more without inc, sl st to next dc, fasten off.

Shape top foot

With RS facing, rejoin blue to 1st dc of 16 dc that are missed, 1 ch, 1 dc in same dc as join, 1 dc in each of next 4 dc, (dec 1 dc) 3 times over next 6 dc, 1 dc in each of next 5 dc, fasten off. With RS facing, rejoin blue to 1st dc of last row, 1 ch, 1 dc in 1st and in each dc to end, fasten off. 13 dc.

Fold top of Foot in half and sew up T-shaped opening.

MUZZLE

Worked in rnds of dc. With natural, make 4 ch, sl st to 1st ch to form circle, 1 ch, 6 dc in circle.

Cont in rnds of dc in spiral and evenly inc 6 dc on next 3 rnds. Work 1 rnd without inc, then inc 6 dc on next rnd as before. 30 dc. Work 1 rnd more on these 30 dc, sl st to next dc, fasten off.

EARS

Make 2 each in natural and blue

With hook, make 4 ch, sl st to 1st ch to form circle, 1 ch, 6 dc in circle, sl st to 1st dc.

Next rnd: 1 ch, 2 dc in each of 6 dc, sl st to 1st dc.

Next rnd: 1 ch, (1 dc, 2 ch, 1 dc) in same dc as sl st, 1 dc in each of next 2 dc, 2 dc in each of next 4 dc, 1 dc in each of next 2 dc, (1 dc, 2 ch, 1 dc) in next dc, 1 dc in each of last 2 dc, sl st to 1st dc.

Next rnd: 1 ch, 1 dc in same dc as sl st, (1 dc, 2 ch, 1 dc) in next 2 ch sp, 1 dc in each of next 5 dc, 2 dc in each of next 4 dc, 1 dc in each of next 5 dc, (1 dc, 2 ch, 1 dc) in next 2 ch sp, 1 dc in each of last 3 dc, sl st to 1st dc, fasten off.

TO MAKE UP

Join Base to lower end of Body, filling when it is half joined. Fill Arms and Legs and attach to Body. Attach Muzzle, filling when it is half joined. Pair up natural and blue Ears, with natural to the front. Sew around outer edges. Attach to Head. Sew on flat buttons for eyes and round button for nose. Embroider mouth with outline stitch. Tie a ribbon around neck. For very young children omit buttons and embroider eyes and nose.

SNOWFLAKE CAT

MATERIALS

Yarn: 8 ply pure new wool 50 g (2 oz) balls; 1$^1/_2$ balls Main Colour (MC); $^1/_4$ ball Contrast (A)
Notions: One set of four 3.25 (3$^1/_4$) mm (No. 10) knitting needles; polyester fibre for filling; 2 buttons for fastening arms; 2 small buttons for eyes; ribbon

MEASUREMENT

Approx 23 cm (9 in) high

SPECIAL ABBREVIATION

M1 = Make 1 stitch: insert right hand needle point from back of work and under horizontal loop before next st, lift it up, then insert left hand needle point in front loop and knit from this position

NOTE

Feet, legs, body and head are worked in one piece

FIRST FOOT AND LEG

With two 3.25 mm (No. 10) needles and MC, cast on 40 sts. Work in st st for 4 rows.
Shape foot
1st row: K18, sl1, K1, psso,TURN.
*2nd row: Sl1, P9, P2 tog, TURN.
3rd row: Sl1, K9, sl1, K1, psso, TURN.
Rep last 2 rows 3 times more, then 2nd row once more, 30 sts rem, then work sl1, knit to end of needle. Beg with purl row work 19 rows straight. Cast/bind off 6 sts at beg of next 2 rows. 18 sts *.

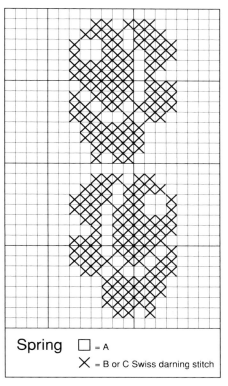

Spring ☐ = A
✗ = B or C Swiss darning stitch

Break off yarn and leave sts on needle.
SECOND FOOT AND LEG
Work as for First Foot and Leg until 4 rows
of st st from beg have been worked.
Shape foot
1st row: K31, sl1, K1, psso, TURN.
Work as for 1st one from * to *. Do not
break yarn. Leave work aside.
CROTCH
With 2 needles and MC, cast on 4 sts.
Work in st st. Inc 1 st each end of 3rd row,
then on every foll 4th row twice more. 10
sts. Work 3 rows straight ending on WS
row, break off yarn, then slip these 10 sts
onto end of 2nd Leg. Ret to beg of 2nd Leg
and cont for Body as follows:
1st rnd: With 1st needle K15, with 2nd
needle K3, then K10 over Crotch, then K3
from other Leg, with 3rd needle K15, then
pick up 4 sts along right hand side of cast-
on edge of Crotch. 50 sts.
Slip last 2 sts of 3rd needle onto 4th
needle. First st of these 2 sts is beg of rnd
and is centre back. 1st 2 sts for next rnd
are already worked. Knit 1 rnd.

*Spring Cardigan is knitted following the
instructions on page 31 and embroidered with the floral motif illustrated
above*

Next rnd: K5, (M1, K8) 5 times, M1, K5. 56 sts.

Knit 1 rnd.

Shape base of body

1st row: K14, then slip last 14 sts of 3rd needle onto other end of same needle. Divide rem 28 sts evenly onto 2 other needles and leave for Front. Ret to 28 sts on 1 needle and work in st st by working to and fro.

Beg with purl row work 11 rows for Base, ending with WS row.

To turn for back

1st row: K17, K2 tog, K1, TURN.

2nd row: P8, P2 tog, P1, TURN.

3rd row: K9, K2 tog, K1, TURN.

4th row: P10, P2 tog, P1, TURN.

5th row: K11, K2 tog, K1, TURN.

6th row: P12, P2 tog, P1, TURN.

Cont in this way by working 1 st more before 2 sts tog each time and always work 1 st before turning until all sts are worked on 1 needle and 18 sts rem, ending with WS row, TURN, then K9 sts. The last st of these 9 sts is end of rnd. Slip 28 sts for Front onto 1 needle. Using another needle K9 for Back. The first st of these 9 sts is beg of rnd and is centre back. With same needle pick up 11 sts along side of base, then with 2nd needle K28 for Front, with 3rd needle pick up 11 sts along other side of Base, then K9 from needle. 68 sts. There should be 20 sts on each of 1st and 3rd needles and 28 sts on 2nd needle.

Always keep first st of rnd at beg of 1st needle.

Cont in rnds as follows:

1st rnd: Knit.

2nd rnd: Knit to last 4 sts of 1st needle, K2 tog, K2, K28 over 2nd needle, over 3rd needle work K2, sl1, K1, psso, knit to end. Rep last 2 rnds 3 times more. 60 sts. Slip 4 sts at each end of 2nd needle onto 1st and 3rd needles. There should be 20 sts on each needle. Knit 1 rnd.

Shape back opening

Turning at end of each row cont as follows:

1st row: Inc 1 st in first st, knit to last st, inc 1 st in last st. 62 sts. TURN.

2nd row: P62, TURN.

3rd row: K62, TURN.

Rep last 2 rows 7 times, then 2nd row once more, then knit 1 row and dec 1 st at each end of row. 60 sts.

Cont in rnds of st st as before. Work 4 rnds.

Shape neck

Evenly dec 10 sts on next and every foll 2nd rnd until 30 sts rem. Work 2 rnds on rem 30 sts.

Next rnd: (K1 tbl) rep to end.

Cont for Head as follows:

Evenly inc 15 sts on every 3rd rnd twice by working M1 to inc and keeping first st of rnd at beg of 1st needle as before. Work 2 rnds straight on these 60 sts.

Next rnd: K21, (K1, M1) 6 times, K6, (M1, K1) 6 times, K21. 72 sts.

Work 10 rnds straight.

Next rnd: K21, (K2 tog) 6 times, K6, (sl1, K1, psso) 6 times, K21. 60 sts.

Work 14 rnds on these rem 60 sts, then evenly dec 10 sts on next and every foll 2nd rnd until 10 sts rem. Work 1 rnd, then break off, leaving a length of yarn. Thread end through rem 10 sts, draw up tightly and securely fasten off.

RIGHT PAW AND ARM

With 2 needles and A, cast on 5 sts. Work in st st. Inc 1 st each end of 1st, 3rd and 5th rows. 11 sts.

Work 5 rows straight *. Break off and leave aside. Using MC work same to *.

**With MC cont for upper section as follows:

1st row: Sl1, K1, psso, K8, M1, K1, then cont to work over A piece as follows: K1, M1, K8, K2 tog. 22 sts.

2nd row: Purl.

3rd row: Sl1, K1, psso, K8, M1, K2, M1, K8, K2 tog.

4th row: Purl.

Rep last 2 rows once. Work 8 rows straight.

Next row: K1, M1, K8, K2 tog, sl1, K1, psso, K8, M1, K1.

Work 3 rows straight.

Rep last 4 rows twice.

Shape top

1st row: (Sl1, K1, psso, K7, K2 tog) twice.

2nd, 4th rows: Purl.

3rd row: (Sl1, K1, psso, K5, K2 tog) twice.

5th row: (Sl1, K1, psso, K3, K2 tog) twice.

Cast/bind off purlwise.

LEFT PAW AND ARM

Work as for Right Paw and Arm, reversing colours for Paw.

SOLES

Make 2

With 2 needles and A, cast on 5 sts. Work in st st. Inc 1 st each end of 1st and 3rd rows, then on foll 6th row once. 11 sts.

Work 9 rows straight, then dec 1 st each end of next 2 rows.

Next rows: K2 tog, cast/bind off to last 2 sts, K2 tog and cast/bind off.

EARS

Make 2 each in MC and A

With 2 needles cast on 16 sts. Work 2 rows in st st. Dec 1 st each end of next and every foll 2nd row until 2 sts rem, then cast/bind off.

TAIL

With 2 needles and MC, cast on 18 sts. Work in st st for 4 rows, then evenly dec 3 sts on next and every foll 6th row until 3 sts rem, then break off, leaving a length of yarn. Thread end through rem 3 sts, draw

up tightly and stitch around to secure. Then with same yarn cont to sew seam.

TO MAKE UP

Sew inside leg seams, then join cast/bind off edge of Leg onto each side of Crotch. Sew Soles in place. Fill firmly and push the filling with point of needle for better shaping. Close back opening. Leaving 3 cm (1¼ in) around top edge of Arm, sew edge of Arms. Fill Arms. Insert button in top of each Arm to secure stitches, then with thick cotton securely attach Arms through Body and through buttons, then close openings. Using one piece each of MC and A sew outer edges of Ears, and attach them to Head. Lightly fill Tail and attach securely in position. Sew on 2 small buttons for eyes, then embroider nose and mouth with A and stitch claws. Tie ribbon around neck and also on tail if desired.

LEO THE LION

HEAD AND BODY

Worked in rnds of dc. Wind gold yarn twice around index finger of left hand for base loop, insert hook in base loop, yoh and draw through. Keeping base loop firm with 2 fingers of left hand work 1 ch, then 6 dc in base loop. Draw up end of yarn tightly to close base loop, sl st to 1st dc.

On next rnd work 1 ch, then 2 dc in each of 6 dc, sl st to 1st dc.

Next rnd: 1 ch, 1 dc in same dc as sl st, (2 dc in next dc, 1 dc in next dc) 5 times, 2 dc in last dc, do not work sl st to join rnd.

Place marker in 1st dc of last rnd to denote

MATERIALS

Yarn: 8 ply pure wool 50 g (2 oz) balls: 2½ balls gold; ½ ball natural; ½ ball brown

Notions: One 3.50 (3½) mm (No. 9) crochet hook; polyester fibre for filling; 2 flat buttons for eyes; 1 round button for nose; dark brown and red wool for embroidery; thin plastic bag; 5 cm x 15 cm (2 in x 6 in) cardboard

MEASUREMENT

25.5 cm (10 in) high

---

beg of rnd. Cont in rnds of dc in spiral, evenly inc 6 dc on every rnd taking care to inc at different positions on each rnd*.

Cont to inc as given until there are 54 dec, then cont to work 9 rnds straight on these 54 dc. Evenly dec 6 dc on next rnd. 48 dc. Work 4 rnds on these rem 48 dc, taking care to dec at different positions on each rnd. Evenly dec 6 dc on every rnd until 24 dc rem.

Next rnd: Sl st in every dc to end.

Next rnd: 1 ch, covering sl st work 1 dc in each dc to end, sl st to 1st dc.

Next rnd: 1 ch, 1 dc in each dc to end, do not work sl st to join rnd.

Place marker in 1st dc of last rnd to denote beg of rnd. Cont in rnds of dc in spiral. Work 1 rnd. Taking care to inc at different position each time evenly inc 6 dc on every rnd until there are 48 dc.

Cont in rnds of dc as before for further 17 rnds, sl st to next dc, fasten off.

BASE

Work as for Head to *, cont to inc as given until there are 48 dc. Work 1 rnd more without inc, sl st to next dc, fasten off.

ARMS

Make 2

Worked in rnds of dc. Wind natural twice

around index finger of left hand for base loop, insert hook in base loop, yoh and draw through, 1 ch. Keeping base loop firm with 2 fingers of left hand work 6 dc in base loop. Draw up end of yarn tightly to close base loop, sl st to 1st dc.

On next rnd work 1 ch, then 2 dc in each dc to end. 12 dc. Cont in rnds in spiral. Work 3 rnds, sl st to next dc, fasten off. Join gold to a dc, and work 1 rnd. Evenly inc 4 dc on next rnd. 16 dc.

Work 10 rnds in spiral on these 16 dc as before, sl st to next dc, fasten off.

FOOT AND LEG

Make 2

Worked in rnds of dc, beginning at centre of sole. With natural, make 7 ch.

1st rnd: 1 dc in 2nd ch from hook, 1 dc in each of next 4 ch, 5 dc in last ch, working on other side of ch work 1 dc in each of next 4 ch, 4 dc in same place as 1st dc, sl st to 1st dc. 18 dc.

2nd rnd: 1 ch, 1 dc in each dc to end at same time inc 3 dc around each curve, sl st to 1st dc.

3rd rnd: As 2nd rnd. 30 dc. Fasten off.

4th rnd: Join gold to centre dc at a curve, 1 ch, 1 dc in same dc as join, 1 dc in each dc to end, sl st to 1st dc, place marker in

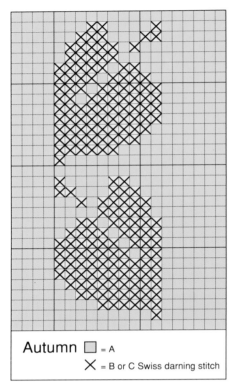

Autumn □ = A
✕ = B or C Swiss darning stitch

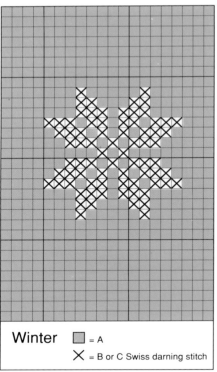

Winter ▨ = A
✕ = B or C Swiss darning stitch

Autumn and Winter Cardigans are knitted following the instructions on page 31 and embroidered with the motifs above

38

last dc of this rnd to denote end of rnd. Cont in rnds of dc in spiral and work 4 rnds.

Shape foot

1st rnd: 1 dc in each of 1st 7 dc, make 4 ch, miss next 16 dc, 1 dc in each of last 7 dc.

2nd rnd: 1 dc in each of 7 dc, then in each of 4 ch, and in each of 7 dc. 18 dc.

Place marker in last dc to denote end of rnd. Cont in rnds in spiral. Work 2 rnds more, then evenly inc 6 dc on next rnd, and on foll 4th rnd once more. 30 dc.

Work 2 rnds more on these 30 dc, sl st to next dc, fasten off.

Cont for top of instep as follows:

With RS facing, join gold to 1st dc of 16 dc that are missed, 1 ch, 1 dc in same dc as join, 1 dc in each of next 4 dc, (dec 1 dc) 3 times over next 6 dc, 1 dc in each of next 5 dc, fasten off.

With RS facing, join gold to 1st dc of last row, 1 ch, 1 dc in same dc as join, 1 dc in each dc to end, fasten off. 13 dc rem.

Matching dc to dc sew top of instep in T-shape.

MUZZLE

Make 2

Worked in rnds of dc. Wind natural twice round the index finger of left hand for base loop, insert hook in this loop, yoh and draw through, 1 ch. Keeping base loop firm with two fingers work 6 dc in base loop. Draw up end of yarn tightly to close base loop, sl st to 1st dc. Cont in spiral and evenly inc 6 dc on next 3 rnds.

Work 2 rnds on these 24 dc without inc, sl st to next dc, fasten off.

Join 2 pieces tog by 4 dc.

EARS

Make 2 each in natural and gold

Work as Muzzle until 12 dc on 2nd rnd have been worked.

3rd rnd: 1 ch, (1 dc, 2 ch, 1 dc) in same dc as sl st, 1 dc in each of next 2 dc, 2 dc in each of next 4 dc, 1 dc in each of next 2 dc, (1 dc, 2 ch, 1 dc) in next dc, 1 dc in each of last 2 dc, sl st to 1st dc.

4th rnd: 1 ch, 1 dc in same dc as sl st, (1 dc, 2 ch, 1 dc) in next ch sp, 1 dc in each of next 5 dc, 2 dc in each of next 4 dc, 1 dc in each of next 5 dc, (1 dc, 2 ch, 1 dc) in next ch sp, 1 dc in each of last 3 dc, sl st to 1st dc.

5th rnd: 1 ch, 1 dc in same dc, 1 dc in each dc to end AT SAME TIME work (1 dc, 2 ch, 1 dc) in ch sp at each of 2 corners, sl st to 1st dc.

Fasten off.

TAIL

With gold, make 8 ch, sl st to 1st ch to form circle, 1 ch, 1 dc in each of 8 ch, sl st to 1st dc. Cont in rnds of dc in spiral until tail is 7 cm (2³/₄ in), sl st to next dc, fasten off.

TO MAKE UP

Join Base to lower end of Body, filling when it is half joined. Fill Arms and Legs. Attach to Body. Attach Muzzle to front of Head, filling when it is half joined. Pair up natural and gold Ear pieces, with natural to the front. Sew around outer edges. Attach Ears to Head.

To make Mane: Wind brown yarn around 5 cm (2 in) side of cardboard until it is covered, keeping it even and not too tight. Carefully slip yarn off cardboard into thin plastic bag and machine stitch down centre, making two rows of loops. Make 7 or 8 such pieces. Position loops under the lion's chin and all over back of head. Sew in place with matching wool.

Sew on 2 buttons for eyes and round button for nose. Embroider French knots on both sides of Muzzle. With red wool embroider mouth at lower seam of Muzzle. Make a tassel and attach to one end of Tail. Attach Tail in position.

CAP

MATERIALS

Yarn: 5 ply pure wool crepe 50 g (2 oz) balls: 1½ balls slate green (A); small quantity sandy brown (B) and natural (C)

Notions: Set of four 3.75 (3¾) mm (No. 9) knitting needles; one 2.8 cm (1⅛ in) self-cover button for top; two 1.9 cm (¾ in) self-cover buttons for chin strap

MEASUREMENT

To fit head 48 cm to 51 cm (19 in to 20 in)

EAR PIECE

With 2 needles from set of 4 and A, cast on 11 sts.

1st row: K1, (P1, K1) 5 times.

2nd row: P1, (K1, P1) 5 times.

Rep last 2 rows twice.

7th row: (K1, P1) twice, (K1 in front and back of loop) in each of next 3 sts, (P1, K1) twice.

8th row: (P1, K1) twice, P6, (K1, P1) twice.

9th row: (K1, P1) twice, inc 1 st in next st, knit to last 5 sts, inc 1 st in next st, (P1, K1) twice.

10th row: (P1, K1) twice, purl to last 4 sts, (K1, P1) twice.

11th to 27th rows: Rep 9th and 10th rows 8 times, then 9th row once more. 34 sts*. Break off yarn. Make another one the same to *, work one row, ending with RS row, then cont as follows:

Next row: With WS facing, (P1, K1) twice, purl to last 4 sts, (K1, P1) twice, with RS facing cast on 23 sts for back, facing WS of other Ear piece work (P1, K1) twice, purl to last 4 sts, (K1, P1) twice.

Next row: (K1, P1) twice, K26, (P1, K1) 15 times, P1, K26, (P1,K1) twice.

Next row: (P1, K1) twice, P26, (K1, P1) 15 times, K1, P26, (K1, P1) twice.

Rep last 2 rows twice more, then with RS facing, using 4 needles as required, cast on 37 sts for front and with RS facing cont in rnds as follows:

1st rnd: (P1, K1) 20 times, P1, K26, (P1,

K1) 15 times, P1, K26, (P1, K1) twice. 128 sts. Catch sts to join in rnd at this point. Rep 1st rnd 3 times.

5th rnd: (P1, K1) 20 times, P1, K83, (P1, K1) twice.

Rep 5th rnd 5 times.

11th rnd: Knit to end.

Rep 11th rnd until front section meas 12 cm (4¾ in) from cast-on edge.

Shape top

1st rnd: (K14, K2 tog) 8 times.

2nd and each alt rnd: Knit.

3rd rnd: (K13, K2 tog) 8 times.

5th rnd: (K12, K2 tog) 8 times.

Cont to dec 8 sts evenly in this way, working 1 st less before each K2 tog on every foll 2nd rnd until 24 sts rem. Knit 1 rnd, then break off keeping length of yarn attached.

Thread end of yarn through rem 24 sts and draw up tightly and securely fasten off.

COVER FOR LARGER BUTTON

With 2 needles from set of 4 and B, cast on 10 sts. Work in st st, inc 1 st each end of 1st and 3rd rows. 14 sts.

Work 11 rows straight, then dec 1 st each end of next and foll 2nd row once more. Cast/bind off purlwise on next row.

COVER FOR SMALLER BUTTONS

With 2 needles from set of 4 and B, cast on

6 sts. Work in st st, inc 1 st each end of 1st and 3rd rows. 10 sts.

Work 5 rows, then dec 1 st each end of next and foll 2nd row once more. Cast/bind off purlwise on next row.

CHIN STRAP

With 2 needles from set of 4 and A, cast on 4 sts.

1st row: K4, then with RS facing push work to other end of same needle and take yarn across back of work to start next row. Always with RS of work facing, rep 1st row until piece meas 23 cm (9 in), then cast/bind off.

TO FINISH OFF

With C and a wool sewing needle, embroider motifs from Graph around head and on each Ear piece. Fold Chin strap in half and sew together side by side, leaving looped end open for buttoning. Attach one end of strap to outside of Ear piece. Attach one smaller button, through all thickness, over strap and other smaller button on other Ear piece to match. Attach larger button to centre top.

Best of Friends

Every little girl would love a best friend like Jemima. They share games and secrets and even have the same taste in clothes!

SNOWDROP JUMPER AND CROCHET SKIRT

JUMPER
BACK

With 3.00 mm (No. 11) needles, cast on 79 (85, 93, 99) sts. Work in K1, P1 rib for 4 (4, 5, 5) cm [1$^1/_2$ (1$^1/_2$, 2, 2) in], ending with WS row. Change to 3.75 mm (No. 9) needles and st st. Cont until work meas 14 (16, 18, 21) cm [5$^1/_2$ (6$^1/_4$, 7, 8$^1/_4$) in] from beg, ending with WS row. Adjust length at this point if required, ending with WS row.

Beg lace patt

1st row: K22 (25, 29, 32) sts, *yfwd, sl1, K2 tog, psso, yfwd, K1, rep from * 7 times more, yfwd, sl1, K2 tog, psso, yfwd, K22 (25, 29, 32) sts.

2nd and each alt rows: Purl.

3rd, 5th rows: K22 (25, 29, 32) sts, *yfwd, sl1, K2 tog, psso, yfwd, K5, rep from * 3 times more, yfwd, sl1, K2 tog, psso, yfwd, K22 (25, 29, 32) sts.

7th row: K22 (25, 29, 32) sts, *K3, yfwd, sl1, K1, psso, K1, K2 tog, yfwd, rep from * 3 times more, K25 (28, 32, 35) sts.

8th row: Purl.

Rep last 8 rows for lace patt for rem. Continue until work meas 20 (22, 24, 27) cm [8 (8$^1/_2$, 9$^1/_2$, 10$^1/_2$) in] from beg or as length adjusted, ending with WS row. Keeping patt correct, cont as follows:

Shape armholes

Cast/bind off 3 (3, 4, 4) sts at beg of next 2 rows. Dec 1 st each end of every row 3 times, then on every foll 2nd row until 59 (63, 67, 71) sts rem. Cont on these rem sts without further dec until work meas 29 (32, 36, 40) cm [11$^1/_2$ (12$^1/_2$, 14, 15$^3/_4$) in] from beg or as length adjusted, ending with WS row.

Shape neck and shoulder

1st row: Patt 21 (23, 24, 25) sts, TURN.

2nd, 4th, 6th rows: P2 tog, purl to end.

3rd row: Patt to end without dec.

5th row: Cast/bind off 6 (6, 7, 8) sts, patt to end.

7th row: Cast/bind off 6 (7, 7, 7) sts, patt to end.

Purl 1 row, then cast/bind off rem 6 (7, 7, 7) sts on next row.

Ret to rem sts, slip centre 17 (17, 19, 21) sts on stitch holder, rejoin yarn at neck edge and finish to match other side.

MATERIALS

Yarn: For Jumper: 5 ply pure wool crepe 50 g (2 oz) balls: 4 (5, 5$^1/_2$, 6) balls

Notions: One pair each 3.75 (3$^3/_4$) mm (No. 9) and 3.00 (3) mm (No. 11) knitting needles; set of four 3.00 (3) mm (No. 11) knitting needles; 6 mm ($^1/_4$ in) wide ribbon; stitch holders

For Skirt: 3$^1/_2$ (4$^1/_2$, 5, 6) balls lilac; 1 (1, 1, 1$^1/_2$) balls white; one each of 3.50 (3$^1/_2$) mm (No. 9) and 3.00 (3) mm (No. 11) crochet hooks; elastic for waist

MEASUREMENTS

Jumper:

To fit underarm
51 (56, 61, 66) cm
20 (22, 24, 26) in

Garment measures
56 (61, 66, 71) cm
22 (24, 26, 28) in

Length   30 (33, 37, 41) cm
11$^3/_4$ (13, 14$^1/_2$, 16) in

Sleeve seam
20 (23, 28, 33) cm
8 (9, 11, 13) in

Skirt:

To fit waist 51 (54, 57, 60) cm
20 (21$^1/_2$, 22$^1/_2$, 23$^1/_2$) in

Length   21 (26, 31, 36) cm
8$^1/_4$ (10$^1/_4$, 12$^1/_4$, 14$^1/_4$) in

TENSION

For jumper: 27 sts and 36 rows to 10 cm (4 in) over st st, using 3.75 mm (No. 9) needles.

For skirt: 17 tr to 8 cm (3$^1/_8$ in) and 10 rows of tr to 9 cm (3$^1/_2$ in), using 3.50 mm (No. 9) hook. It is important to knit a tension square and to work to the stated tension in order to obtain the required measurements. If your square is bigger use finer needles. If your square is smaller use thicker needles.

SPECIAL ABBREVIATIONS

(1 dc, 2 ch) at beg of tr row stands for 1 tr, and always work last tr on next row into top of (1 dc, 2 ch)

dec 1 tr = decrease 1 tr: (yoh, insert hook in next tr, yoh and draw through, yoh and draw through 2 loops on hook) twice, yoh and draw through 3 loops on hook

FRONT

Work as for Back until work meas 24 (27, 30, 34) cm [9$^1/_2$ (10$^1/_2$, 11$^3/_4$, 13$^1/_2$) in] from beg or as length adjusted, ending with WS row.

Keeping patt correct, cont as follows:

Shape neck

1st row: Patt 25 (27, 28, 29) sts, TURN. Cont on these 25 (27, 28, 29) sts. Cast/bind off 2 sts at beg of next row and foll 2nd row once more, then dec 1 st at neck edge on every foll 2nd row 3 times. Cont on rem 18 (20, 21, 22) sts until work meas same as Back to shoulder, ending at armhole edge.

Shape shoulder

Cast/bind off at beg of next and each alt row 6 (6, 7, 8) sts once, 6 (7, 7, 7) sts twice. Return to rem sts, slip centre 9 (9, 11, 13) sts on stitch holder, rejoin yarn at neck edge and finish to match other side.

SLEEVES

With 3.00 mm (No. 11) needles, cast on 39 (41, 43, 45) sts. Work in K1, P1 rib for 4 (4, 5, 5) cm [1$^1/_2$ (1$^1/_2$, 2, 2) in], ending with RS row.

Inc row: Rib 7 (8, 7, 9) sts, *inc 1 st in next st, rib 7 (7, 8, 8) sts, rep from *, ending with rib 7 (8, 8, 8) sts in last rep. 43 (45, 47, 49) sts.

Change to 3.75 mm (No. 9) needles and cont as follows:

1st row: K16 (17, 18, 19) sts, *yfwd, sl1, K2 tog, psso, yfwd, K1, rep from * once, yfwd, sl1, K2 tog, psso, yfwd, K16 (17, 18, 19) sts.

2nd and each alt row: Purl.

3rd, 5th rows: K16 (17, 18, 19) sts, yfwd, sl1, K2 tog, psso, yfwd, K5, yfwd, sl1, K2 tog, psso, yfwd, K16 (17, 18, 19) sts.

7th row: K1, inc 1 st in next st, K17 (18, 19, 20) sts, yfwd, sl1, K1, psso, K1, K2 tog, yfwd, knit to last 2 sts, inc 1 st in next st, K1. Rep last 8 rows for lace patt AT SAME TIME inc 1 st each end as shown on 7th row on every foll 6th (6th, 8th, 8th) row 3 (3, 4, 5) times, then on every foll 6th row (all sizes) until there are 59 (65, 69, 75) sts, taking all inc sts into st st. Cont straight until work meas 20 (23, 28, 33) cm [8 (9, 11, 13) in] from beg, ending with WS row. Adjust length at this point if required.

Shape top

Keeping lace patt correct, cast/bind off 3 (3, 4, 4) sts at beg of next 2 rows, then dec 1 st each end of every row 3 times, then on every foll 2nd row until 21 (23, 23, 27) sts rem. Purl 1 row, then cast/bind off 2 sts at beg of next 6 rows, then rem 9 (11, 11, 15) sts on next row.

TO MAKE UP
Lightly press on wrong side. Sew shoulder seams.

NECKBAND
With RS facing and set of four 3.00 mm (No. 11) needles, pick up and knit 25 (26, 27, 27) sts on each side of front neck, K9 (9, 11, 13) sts at centre front, 7 sts on each side of back neck, K17 (17, 19, 21) sts from centre back neck. 90 (92, 98, 102) sts. Work 8 rnds in K1, P1 rib.

Next rnd: *K1, yrn, P1, yon, rep from * to end.

Next rnd: *K1, (P1, K1) in next loop, P1, (K1, P1) in next loop, rep from * to end. Work in rnds of K1, P1 as before for further 8 rnds. Loosely cast off in rib.

TO FINISH OFF
Sew up side and sleeve seams. Set sleeves smoothly into armholes. Thread ribbon through holes of Neckband and tie at centre front.

SKIRT
BACK AND FRONT ALIKE
With 3.50 mm (No. 9) hook, make 111 (131, 153, 173) ch.

1st row: 1 tr in 4th ch from hook, 1 tr in each ch to end. 109 (129, 151, 171) tr, counting 3 ch as 1 tr.

2nd row: (1 dc, 2 ch) in 1st tr, 1 tr in each tr, ending with last tr in top of 3 ch.

3rd row: (1 dc, 2 ch) in 1st tr, 1 tr in each tr to end.

Rep last row twice.

1st dec row: (1 dc, 2 ch) in 1st tr, 1 tr in each of next 3 (7, 8, 7) tr, *dec 1 tr, 1 tr in

each of next 7 (6, 9, 9) tr, rep from * 11 (14, 12, 14) times more, ending with 1 tr in each of last 4 (7, 8, 7) tr instead of 7 (6, 9, 9) tr. 97 (114, 138, 156) tr.

Work 3 (5, 5, 5) rows without dec.

2nd dec row: (1 dc, 2 ch) in 1st tr, 1 tr in each of next 8 (6, 7, 9) tr, *dec 1 tr, 1 tr in each of next 5 (5, 8, 7) tr, rep from * 11 (14, 12, 15) times more, ending with 1 tr in each of last 9 (7, 8, 9) tr instead of 5 (5, 8, 7) tr. 85 (99, 125, 140) tr.

Work 3 (3, 5, 5) rows without dec.

3rd dec row: (1 dc, 2 ch) in 1st tr, 1 tr in each of next 2 (7, 7, 8) tr, *dec 1 tr, 1 tr in each of next 5 (7, 7, 6) tr, rep from * 11 (9, 12, 15) times more, ending with 1 tr in each of last 3 (8, 7, 9) tr instead of 5 (7, 7, 6) tr. 73 (89, 112, 124) tr rem.

Work 3 (3, 3, 5) rows without dec.

4th dec row: (1 dc, 2 ch) in 1st tr, 1 tr in each of next 3 (7, 6, 8) tr, *dec 1 tr, 1 tr in each of next 5 (6, 6, 5) tr, rep from * 9 (9, 12, 15) times more, ending with 1 tr in each of last 4 (7, 7, 8) tr instead of 5 (6, 6, 5) tr. 63 (79, 99, 108) tr.

Cont for 2nd, 3rd and 4th sizes only as follows:
Work (3, 3, 5) rows without dec.

5th dec row: (1 dc, 2 ch) in 1st tr, 1 tr in each of next (6, 6, 7) tr, *dec 1 tr, 1 tr in each of next (5, 5, 4) tr, rep from * (9, 12, 15) times more, ending with 1 tr in each of last (7, 6, 8) tr instead of (5, 5, 4) tr. (69, 86, 92) tr.

Cont for 3rd and 4th sizes only as follows:
Work (3, 5) rows without dec.

6th dec row: (1 dc, 2 ch) in 1st tr, 1 tr in each of next (5, 2) tr, *dec 1 tr, 1 tr in each

of next (4, 4) tr, rep from * (12, 14) times more, ending with 1 tr in each of last (6, 3) tr instead of (4, 4) tr. (73, 77) tr.

Cont for all sizes as follows:
Cont on rem 63 (69, 73, 77) tr without further dec until work measures 18 (23, 28, 33) cm [7 (9, 11, 13) in] from beg. There will be 3 cm (1⅛ in) wide Waistband added to this measurement for a total skirt length. Adjust length at this point if required. Fasten off. Make other half the same.

TO MAKE UP
Lightly press on wrong side. With a fine backstitch sew up side seams.

WAISTBAND
With 3.00 mm (No. 11) hook and RS facing, join yarn to top edge at a side seam, 1 ch, 1 dc in each tr round top edge to end, sl st to 1st dc, TURN.

Next 3 rnds: 3 ch, 1 tr in each dc to end, sl st to top of 3 ch, TURN.

Next rnd: (RS) 3 ch, *1 ch, miss 1 tr, insert hook from back of work then pass in front of next tr, then through to back of work, yoh and draw through, (yoh and draw through 2 loops on hook) twice – 1 trF is made, rep from * to last tr, 1 ch, miss 1 tr, sl st to top of 3 ch, TURN.

Next rnd: 4 ch, *1 tr in next tr, 1 ch, rep from * to end, ending with 1 ch, sl st to 3rd of 4 ch.

Rep last rnd once more, fasten off.

TO FINISH OFF
Cut elastic to waist size and join ends tog

to form circle. Place elastic inside Waistband. Fold 3 rnds of Waistband to inside over elastic and stitch down.

Frill: With RS facing and 3.00 mm (No. 11) hook, join white to lower edge at a side seam, 4 ch, 1 tr in same place as join, (1 tr, 1 ch, 1 tr) in each foundation ch around lower edge to end, sl st to 3rd of 4 ch.

Next rnd: Sl st to 1st ch sp, 4 ch, 1 tr in same sp as 4 ch, (1 tr, 1 ch, 1 tr) in each 1 ch sp to end, sl st to 3rd of 4 ch, fasten off.

JEMIMA

FIRST FOOT AND LEG

With two 3.25 mm (No. 10) needles and black, cast on 44 sts. Work in st st for 4 rows.

Shape foot

1st row: K20, K2 tog tbl, TURN.
***2nd row:** Sl1, P9, P2 tog, TURN.
3rd row: Sl1, K9, K2 tog tbl, TURN.

Rep last 2 rows 5 times, then 2nd row once more. 30 sts. Break yarn, TURN, then slip all sts onto left needle. With RS facing, join black to first st. Work over all sts for 2 rows. Change to natural and work 38 rows. Cast/bind off 6 sts at beg of next 2 rows. 18 sts*. Break off yarn and leave sts on needle.

SECOND FOOT AND LEG

Work as for First Foot and Leg until 4 rows of st st from beg have been worked.

Shape foot

1st row: K33, K2 tog tbl, TURN.
Work as for 1st one from * to *. Do not

break yarn. Leave work aside.

CROTCH

With 2 needles and natural, cast on 6 sts. Work 12 rows in st st. Break yarn. With RS facing, slip these 6 sts to end of Second Leg. Ret to beg of Second Leg and cont for Body as follows:

Next row: With 1st needle K13, with 2nd needle K5, K6 over Crotch, then K5 from other Leg, with 3rd needle K13, pick up 6 sts along RS of cast-on edge of Crotch. 48 sts.

Slip last 3 sts onto 4th needle. The first st of 4th needle is beg of rnd and is centre back. First 3 sts for next rnd are already worked. Cont in rnds of st st by knitting every rnd. Work 2 rnds.

Next rnd: K2, (M1, K4) rep to last 2 sts, M1, K2. 60 sts.
Work 6 rnds straight.

Make back opening

Next rnd: Inc 1 st in first st, knit to last st, inc 1 st in last st. 62 sts, TURN.
Working in rows, cont on these 62 sts in st st for further 25 rows, ending with WS row. Dec 1 st each end of next row. 60 sts. Cont in rnds of st st as before and work 4 rnds.

Shape for neck

Evenly dec 10 sts on next and every foll 3rd rnd until 30 sts rem. Work 2 rnds straight.

Next rnd: (K1 tbl) rep to end.
Cont for Head as follows:
Cont in rnds of st st and evenly inc 15 sts on every foll 3rd rnd twice. 60 sts, then evenly inc 12 sts on foll 3rd rnd. 72 sts. Work 4 rnds straight.

Shape mouth

Next rnd: K34, inc 1 st in each of next 4 sts, K34. 76 sts.
Work 2 rnds straight.

Next rnd: K42, turn, P8, TURN, K42 to complete rnd.

Next rnd: K34, (K2 tog) 4 times, K34. 72 sts.
Work 3 rnds straight.

Shape cheeks

Next rnd: K21, (K2 tog) 6 times, K6, (sl1, K1, psso) 6 times, K21. 60 sts.
Keeping beg of rnd at beg of 1st needle as before, rearrange sts evenly on 3 needles. Cont in st st, work 12 rnds straight, then evenly dec 10 sts on next and every foll 2nd rnd until 10 sts rem. Work 1 rnd on rem 10 sts. Break off, leaving a length of yarn attached. Thread end of yarn through rem 10 sts, draw end of yarn up tightly and securely fasten off.

HANDS AND ARMS

With 2 needles and natural, cast on 2 sts. Work in st st, inc 1 st each end of 1st and 3rd rows. 6 sts. Work 3 rows straight*. Break yarn. Leave aside. Make another piece the same to * and cont as follows:

Next row: Cast on 3 sts and knit these 3 sts, K6, then K6 from other piece.
Next row: Cast on 3 sts, purl all sts. 18 sts.
Next row: Sl1, K1, psso, K6, M1, K2, M1, K6, K2 tog.
Next row: Purl.
Rep last 2 rows twice, then work 2 rows straight. Inc 1 st each end of next row. 20 sts. Work 11 rows straight.

Next row: K1, M1, K7, K2 tog, sl1, K1, psso, K7, M1, K1.
Work 3 rows straight, then rep these last 4 rows twice.

Shape top

1st row: (Sl1, K1, psso, K6, K2 tog) twice.
2nd, 4th, 6th rows: Purl.
3rd row: (Sl1, K1, psso, K4, K2 tog) twice.
5th row: (Sl1, K1, psso, K2, K2 tog) twice.

MATERIALS

Yarn: For Doll: 8 ply pure wool 50 g (2 oz) balls: $2\frac{1}{2}$ balls natural; $\frac{1}{2}$ ball black

For Dress: 5 ply pure wool crepe 50 g (2 oz) balls: 1 ball lilac; $\frac{1}{2}$ ball white

Notions: Set of four 3.25 ($3\frac{1}{4}$) mm (No. 10) knitting needles for doll; one pair each of 3.75 ($3\frac{3}{4}$) mm (No. 9) and 3.25 ($3\frac{1}{4}$) mm (No. 10) knitting needles for dress; 3 ply pure wool in brown for Hair; polyester fibre for filling; 2 buttons for fastening arms; 4 buttons for dress; small quantity each of red and dark brown for embroidering features; 20 cm x 10 cm (8 in x 4 in) cardboard; thin plastic bag

MEASUREMENT

Approx 41 cm (16 in) high

SPECIAL ABBREVIATION

M1 = make 1 stitch: insert right needle point from back of work and under horizontal loop before next st, lift it up, then insert left needle point in front loop and knit from this position

NOTE

Feet, legs, body and head are worked in one piece

Cast/bind off. Make another one the same.

SOLES

Make 2

With 2 needles and black, cast on 5 sts. Work in st st, inc 1 st each end of 1st and 3rd rows. 9 sts. Inc 1 st each end of foll 8th row twice. 13 sts. Work 3 rows straight, then dec 1 st each end of next and foll 2nd row once more.

Next row: (Toe end) P2 tog, cast/bind off to last 2 sts, P2 tog, cast/bind off.

DRESS

With pair of 3.75 mm (No. 9) needles and lilac, cast on 81 sts. Knit 5 rows.

Next row: K4, *inc 1 st in next st, K8, rep from *, ending with K4 instead of K8. 90 sts. Cont for Skirt section as follows:

1st row: Knit.

2nd row: K5, purl to last 5 sts, K5.

3rd, 4th rows: Rep 1st and 2nd rows.

5th row: K1, K2 tog, yfwd, knit to end. 1st buttonhole is made.

6th to 14th rows: Work 2nd row, then rep 1st and 2nd rows 4 times.

Rep last 14 rows once more.

Next row: K5, K2 tog, K7, *K2 tog, K8, rep from * 5 times more, K2 tog, K7, K2 tog, K5. 81 sts.

Next row: K5, purl to last 5 sts, K5.

Divide for left back yoke

1st row: K17, TURN.

2nd row: Purl to last 5 sts, K5.

3rd row: K1, K2 tog, yfwd, K14. 3rd buttonhole is made.

Work 2nd row, then rep 1st and 2nd rows 4 times, then work 1st row once more, ending at armhole edge.

Next row: P7, TURN, leave rem 10 sts on a piece of wool for Neckband.

Work 4 rows more in st st on these 7 sts. Cast/bind off.

Ret to rem sts, leave next 9 sts on a piece of wool for Sleeve, join lilac to next st, and K29, TURN, then cont on these 29 sts for front yoke and work further 13 rows in st st. On next row K7 and work 3 rows more on these 7 sts, then cast/bind off.

Leave centre 15 sts of front yoke on a piece of wool for Neckband. Join lilac to next st, K7, work 3 rows more in st st, cast/bind off.

Ret to rem sts, leave next 9 sts on a piece of wool for sleeve, join lilac to next st, K17.

Work 13 rows more, ending with WS row. On next row K7, TURN, and leave rem 10 sts on a piece of wool for Neckband. Work 3 rows more in st st on these 7 sts. Cast/bind off.

HINT

Take care to make up your garment or toy neatly for a really professional finish. Check the ball band of your yarn and, if ironing is recommended, press the pieces carefully on the wrong side using a damp cloth. Ribbing and some textured patterns are better left unpressed. Where strength is required in the seams, such as for a stuffed toy, join the pieces together using backstitch. For lighter, lacy garment seams an edge-to-edge seam is ideal.

SLEEVES

With RS facing, 3.75 mm (No. 9) needles and lilac, beg and end at shoulder edge, evenly pick up 16 sts along armhole edge, K9 from piece of wool, pick up 16 sts on other side of armhole edge. 41 sts.

1st and each alt row: Purl.

2nd row: K15, sl1, K1, psso, K7, K2 tog, K15.

4th row: K15, sl1, K1, psso, K5, K2 tog, K15.

6th row: K15, sl1, K1, psso, K3, K2 tog, K15.

8th row: K15, sl1, K1, psso, K1, K2 tog, K15.

Change to 3.25 mm (No. 10) needles. Knit 5 rows. Cast/bind off.

NECKBAND

Sew shoulder seams, then cont to sew sleeve tops. With RS facing, pair of 3.25 mm (No. 10) needles and lilac, K10 from piece of wool on left back yoke, pick up 9 sts on side of neck, K15 from piece of wool at centre front yoke, pick up 9 sts on side of neck, K10 from piece of wool on right back yoke. 53 sts. Knit 1 row.

Next row: K1, K2 tog, yfwd, 4th buttonhole is made, K5, *K2 tog, K5, rep from * 4 times, K2 tog, K8. 47 sts.

Knit 2 rows.

Next row: K11, *K2 tog, K6, rep from * twice, K2 tog, K10. 43 sts.

Knit 1 row. Cast/bind off.

FRILL

With RS facing, 3.25 mm (No. 10) needles and white, pick up 1 st from each cast-on st to end. 81 sts.

1st row: (K1, yfwd) rep to last st, K1.

2nd row: *(K1, P1) in next st, (K1, P1) in next loop which was made by yfwd, rep from * to last st, (K1, P1) in last st.

3rd, 4th rows: (K1, P1) rep to end. Cast/bind off.

TO MAKE UP

Sew side seam of Legs and attach Soles. Join cast/bind off edge of Legs to each side of Crotch. Firmly fill, then with point of knitting needle push filling for better shaping. Close back opening. Leaving 3 cm (1¼ in) around top edge for opening, sew outer edges of Hand and Arms. Fill. Insert button in top edge of each Arm to secure stitches. With thick cotton securely attach arms through the body through buttons. Close openings. Pinch fullness of mouth section and with natural stitch through all thicknesses to form a pouting mouth. With red, embroider around ridge of mouth. With dark brown, embroider eyes as illustrated. With desired colour stitch shoe lace on foot sections.

To make hair: Wind yarn evenly around 20 cm (8 in) length of cardboard until width is covered. Tie off ends. Carefully cut one end to make length of 40 cm (16 in). Keeping shape put hair into thin plastic bag. With the same colour cotton, sew over plastic bag across width of hair at centre. Sew over line twice. Remove plastic bag. Place stitching line as centre parting line on the head, then sew along parting line to secure hair on head and make a curl at centre front. Style and trim hair as desired. Sew 4 buttons on dress.

Classic Kids

This young lad and his highland lassie look a very smart pair in these traditional knits.

COAT OF ARMS JUMPER

MATERIALS

Yarn: 8 ply pure wool 50 g (2 oz) balls: 3 (4, 4, 5) balls Main Colour (MC); 1 (1, 1, 1) ball First Contrast (A) ; 1 (1, 2, 2) ball/s Second Contrast (B) ; small quantity of Third Contrast (C) for embroidery
Notions: One pair each 4.00 (4) mm (No. 8) and 3.25 (3 1/4) mm (No. 10) knitting needles; set of four 3.25 (3 1/4) mm (No. 10) knitting needles; stitch holders

MEASUREMENTS

To fit underarm
	51 (56, 61, 66) cm
	20 (22, 24, 26) in
Garment measures	
	56 (61, 66, 71) cm
	22 (24, 26, 28) in
Length	30 (33, 37, 41) cm
	11 3/4 (13, 14 1/2, 16) in
Sleeve seam	20 (23, 28, 33) cm
	8 (9, 11, 13) in

TENSION

23 sts and 32 rows to 10 cm (4 in) over st st, using 4 mm (No. 8) needles.
It is important to knit a tension square and to work to the stated tension in order to obtain the required measurements. If your square is bigger use finer needles. If your square is smaller use thicker needles.

SPECIAL ABBREVIATION

M1 = Make 1: lift horizontal loop before next st onto left hand needle and K1 on a knit row or P1 on a purl row into this loop, twisting loop to avoid making hole

NOTE

Use separate balls of yarn for each colour section

BACK

Using 3.25 mm (No. 10) needles and MC cast on 67 (73, 77, 83) sts. Work in K1, P1

rib for 4 (4, 5, 5) cm or 1 1/2 (1 1/2, 2, 2) in, ending with WS row. Change to 4 mm (No. 8) needles and st st. Work until Back meas 15 (17, 19, 21) cm [6 (6 3/4 , 7 1/2, 8 1/4) in] from beg, ending with WS row. Adjust length at this point if required, ending with WS row.
Cont as follows:

1st row: K33 (36, 38, 41) sts MC, K1 A, K33 (36, 38, 41) sts MC.
2nd row: P32 (35, 37, 40) sts MC, P3 A, P32 (35, 37, 40) sts MC.
3rd row: K31 (34, 36, 39) sts MC, K5 A, K31 (34, 36, 39) sts MC.
4th row: P30 (33, 35, 38) sts MC, P7 A, P30 (33, 35, 38) sts MC.
5th row: K29 (32, 34, 37) sts MC, K4A, K1B, K4A, K29 (32, 34, 37) sts MC.
6th row: P28 (31, 33, 36) sts MC, P4A, P3B, P4A, P28 (31 33 36) sts MC.
7th row: K27 (30, 32, 35) sts MC, K4A, K5B, K4A, K27 (30, 32, 35) sts MC.
Cont working 1 st less in MC at each end, moving 4 sts in A outwards, and working 2 sts more in B at centre on every row in this way until there are 23 (23, 27, 27) sts in 2 colours at centre of piece.

Shape raglans

Cont until all sts are in B, AT SAME TIME cast/bind off 4 sts at beg of next 2 rows.
Next row: K2 tog, cont colour pattern as before to last 2 sts, sl1, K1, psso.
Next row: Purl in colours as before without dec.
Rep last 2 rows until there are 25 (27, 27, 29) sts rem in all, ending on a purl row. Leave sts on a stitch holder.

FRONT

Work as for Back until there are 41 (43, 45, 49) sts rem in raglan shaping, ending on a purl row.

Shape neck

1st row: K2 tog, knit until there are 15 (15, 17, 18) sts on right hand needle, TURN. Cont on these 15 (15, 17, 18) sts as follows:
2nd row: Cast/bind off 2 (2, 3, 3) sts, purl to end.
3rd row: K2 tog, knit to end.
4th row: Cast/bind off 2 sts (all sizes), purl to end.
Rep last 2 rows once (all sizes), then cont to dec 1 st at raglan edge only on next and every foll 2nd row until 2 sts rem (all sizes). Work 2 sts tog. Fasten off.
Return to rem sts, leave centre 9 (11, 9, 11) sts on a stitch holder, rejoin B to next st and cont for other side of neck as

follows:
1st row: Knit to last 2 sts, sl1, K1, psso.
2nd row: Purl.
3rd row: Cast/bind off 2 (2, 3, 3) sts, knit to last 2 sts, sl1, K1, psso.
4th row: Purl.
5th row: Cast off 2 sts, knit to last 2 sts, sl1, K1, psso.
Rep last 2 rows once, then cont to dec 1 st at raglan edge only until 2 sts rem. Work 2 sts tog. Fasten off.

SLEEVES

Using 3.25 mm (No. 10) needles and MC, cast on 35 (37, 39, 41) sts. Work in K1, P1

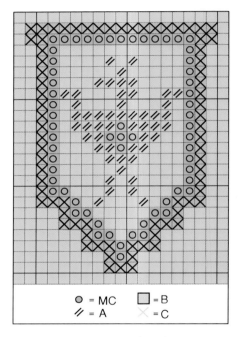

○ = MC   □ = B
/ = A   × = C

rib for 4 (4, 5, 5) cm [1 1/2 (1 1/2, 2, 2) in], ending with WS row and inc 2 sts evenly spaced on last row. 37 (39, 41, 43) sts. Change to 4 mm (No. 8) needles and st st. Work 6 rows.
Next row: K2, M1, knit to last 2 sts, M1, K2.
Cont to inc 1 st by working M1 2 sts from each end on every foll 6th (7th, 7th, 8th) row until there are 51 (55, 59, 63) sts. Cont on these sts without shaping until Sleeve measures 19 (22, 26, 32) cm [7 3/4 (8 1/2, 10 1/4, 12 1/2) in], or length required, ending on WS (RS, RS, WS) row.
Work colour patt as follows:
Place marker in 26th (28th, 30th, 32nd) st from one end to mark centre st and cont as follows:
1st row: With MC, work to centre st, work 1 st in A, with MC work to end.

2nd row: With MC, work to centre 3 sts, with A work 3 sts, with MC work to end. Cont to work in colours as for Back, working 2 (1, 3, 2) more rows, ending on WS row for all sizes.

Shape raglans

Cont to work colours as for Back until all sts are in B, AT SAME TIME cast/bind off 4 sts at beg of next 2 rows, then dec 1 st at each end of next and every foll 2nd row as for Back raglan shaping until 9 sts rem (all sizes), ending with WS row. Leave sts on a stitch holder.

TO MAKE UP

Darn in all ends. Press lightly on wrong side. Sew 4 raglan seams, matching colours. Sew side and sleeve seams.

NECKBAND

With RS facing and using a set of four 3.25 mm (No. 10) needles and B, knit up 9 sts from each sleeve top, 16 (16, 18, 20) sts on each side of front neck, 9 (11, 9, 11) sts on centre front neck, 25 (27, 27, 29) sts on back neck. 84 (88, 90, 98) sts.
Work in rnds of K1, P1 rib for 6 cm (2¹/₂ in). Cast/bind off loosely in rib.

TO FINISH OFF

Fold half Neckband to inside and slipstitch into place. Using Swiss darning (knitting stitch) embroider coat of arms following Graph.

TARTAN VEST

BACK

Using 3.25 mm (No. 10) needles and MC, cast on 63 (69, 75, 81) sts. Work in K1, P1 rib for 3 cm (1¹/₄ in), ending with WS row. Change to 4 00 mm (No. 8) needles and cont in patt as follows:

1st and 2nd rows: With A, knit.
3rd row: With A, knit.
4th row: With A, PO (3, 6, 9) sts, K1, P1, K1, *(P8, K1) twice, P1, K1, rep from * to last 0 (3, 6, 9) sts, P0 (3, 6, 9) sts.
5th to 10th rows: Rep 3rd and 4th rows 3 times.
11th and 12th rows: With A, knit.
13th and 14th rows: With MC, knit.
15th to 22nd rows: With B, rep 3rd and 4th rows 4 times.

MATERIALS

Yarn: 8 ply pure wool crepe 50 g (2 oz) balls: 1 (1¹/₂, 2, 2¹/₂) ball/s Main Colour (MC); 1 (1, 2, 2) ball/s First Contrast (A); 1 (1, 1¹/₂, 2) ball/s Second Contrast (B); small quantity of Third Contrast (C)

Notions: One pair each 4.00 (4) mm (No. 8) and 3.25 (3¹/₄) mm (No. 10) knitting needles; set of four 3.25 (3¹/₄) mm (No. 10) knitting needles; 3.50 (3¹/₂) mm crochet hook; stitch holder; safety pin

MEASUREMENTS

To fit underarm

	51 (56, 61, 66) cm
	20 (22, 24, 26) in
Garment measures	
	56 (61, 66, 71) cm
	22 (24, 26, 28) in
Length	30 (33, 37, 41) cm
	11³/₄ (13, 14¹/₂, 16) in

TENSION

22 sts and 34 rows to 10 cm (4 in) over patt, using 4.00 mm (No. 8) needles. It is important to knit a tension square and to work to the stated tension in order to obtain the required measurements. If your square is bigger use finer needles. If your square is smaller use thicker needles.

23rd and 24th rows: With B, knit.
25th and 26th rows: With MC, knit.
27th to 29th rows: With MC, rep 3rd and 4th rows once, then 3rd row only once more.
30th and 31st rows: With C, purl.
32nd to 34th rows: With MC, purl 1 row, then rep 3rd and 4th rows once.
35th and 36th rows: With MC, knit.
Rep last 36 rows for patt. Cont in patt AT SAME TIME when work meas 18 (19, 21, 24) cm [7 (7¹/₂, 8¹/₄, 9¹/₂) in] from beg, ending on WS row, shape armholes as follows. Adjust length at this point if required, ending with WS row. Keeping patt correct cont as follows:

Shape armholes

Cast off 4 sts (all sizes) at beg of next 2 rows. Dec 1 st each end of every row 3 times, then on every foll 2nd row 3 (4, 4, 5) times. Cont on rem 43 (47, 53, 57) sts without further dec until work meas 30 (33,

37, 41) cm [11³/₄ (13, 14¹/₂, 16) in] from beg, or as length adjusted, ending on WS row.

Shape shoulders

Cast/bind off 3 (5, 5, 6) sts at beg of next 2 rows, then 4 (4, 5, 5) sts at beg of next 4 rows. Leave rem 21 (21, 23, 25) sts on a stitch holder.

To position stripes: Work centre g st in MC, then work toward right side edge *miss 8 sts, next g st in MC, miss 1 st, next garter st in C, miss 8 sts, next g st in MC, rep from * to end. Work toward left side edge **miss 8 sts, next garter st in C, miss 1 st, next g st in MC, miss 8 sts, next g st in MC, rep from ** to end.

To work stripes with hook: Place yarn at wrong side of work, insert hook from right side of work through last row of rib band, *yarn round hook and pull a loop through to right side of work, insert hook in st directly above last st, rep from * to end.

FRONT

Work as for Back to armholes, ending with WS row.
Keeping patt correct

Divide for V neck and shape armhole

1st row: Cast off 4 sts, patt until 27 (30, 33, 36) sts on right needle, TURN.
***Cont on these 27 (30, 33, 36) sts and dec 1 st at armhole edge on next 3 rows, then on every foll 2nd row 3 (4, 4, 5) times. Cont straight at armhole edge, AT SAME TIME dec 1 st at neck edge on every 2nd row 4 times, then on every foll 4th row 6 (6, 7, 8) times.
Cont on rem 11 (13, 15, 16) sts until Front

Midnight, the black cat is knitted following the instructions for Snowflake, the white cat, on page 34

meas same as Back to shoulder, ending at shoulder edge.

Shape shoulder

Cast off at beg of next and each alt row 3 (5, 5, 6) sts once, 4 (4, 5, 5) sts twice. Ret to rem sts, slip centre st onto safety pin. Rejoin yarn at neck edge and work 1 row in patt. Cast off 4 sts at beg of next row, then complete to match other side from ***.

To position stripes: Work centre st in MC, then work toward right side edge from ** of stripe position for Back, then toward left side edge work from * of stripe position for Back.

Work stripes with hook as for Back.

TO MAKE UP

Press lightly on wrong side. Sew shoulder seams. Sew side seams, matching stripes.

NECKBAND

With RS facing, using four 3.25 mm (No. 10) needles and MC, beg at left shoulder seam, evenly pick up and knit 38 (44, 50, 56) sts on left side of front neck, K1 from pin and place marker in this st to denote V point, pick up and knit 38 (44, 50, 56) sts on right side of front neck, 21 (21, 23, 25) sts on back neck. 98 (110, 124, 138) sts.

1st rnd: (K1, P1) rep to end.

2nd rnd: (K1, P1) 18 (21, 24, 27) times, K1, slip next 2 sts tog as if to K2 tog, K1, pass 2 sl sts tog over st just knitted – now 1 st on either side of V point st is decreased behind stitch, (K1, P1) rep to end.

3rd rnd: Rib as before to 1st before V point st, dec as on 2nd rnd, rib to end. Rep last rnd 4 times. Cast/bind off in rib.

ARMHOLE BANDS

With RS facing, a set of four 3.25 mm (No. 10) needles and B, evenly pick up and knit 74 (82, 90, 102) sts around armhole. Work 7 rnds in K1, P1 rib. Cast/bind off in rib.

HINT

Most of the garments in this book are given in several sizes. It is always best to measure your child before beginning to knit a new garment. Little ones grow very quickly and using measurements even a few months old can lead to disappointment and wasted effort.

BERET

MATERIALS

Yarn: 8 ply pure wool crepe 50 g (2 oz) balls: 1 ball green; small quantity each of 3 other colours for Pompom

Notions: One pair 4.00 (4) mm (No. 8) knitting needles; cable needle; 50 cm (20 in) of 6 mm (¼ in) wide flat elastic, joined to form circle

MEASUREMENT

To fit Head 46 cm (18 in) to 51 cm (20 in)

TENSION

22 sts and 32 rows to 10 cm (4 in) over st st, using 4 mm (No. 8) needles. It is important to knit a tension square and to work to the stated tension in order to obtain the required measurements. If your square is bigger use finer needles. If your square is smaller use thicker needles.

SPECIAL ABBREVIATION

C4 = Cable 4 stitches: slip next 2 sts onto cable needle and leave at front of work, K2, then K2 from cable needle

Using 4.00 mm (No. 8) needles and green, cast on 52 sts.

1st row: K14 (P2, K4) twice, K21, TURN.

2nd row: Yrn on right needle, tightening loop in 1st st P25 (K2, P4) twice, K10.

3rd row: K14, P2, C4, P2, K20, TURN.

4th row: Yrn on right needle, tightening loop in 1st st P20 (K2, P4) twice, K10.

5th row: K14, P2, K4, P2, K15, TURN.

6th row: Yrn on right needle, tightening loop in 1st st P15 (K2, P4) twice, K10.

7th row: K14, P2, C4, P2, K10, TURN.

8th row: Yrn on right needle, tightening loop in 1st st P10 (K2, P4) twice, K10.

9th row: K14, P2, K4, P2, K5, TURN.

10th row: Yrn on right needle, tightening loop in 1st st P5 (K2, P4) twice, K10.

11th row: K14, P2, C4, P2, K5 (K2 tog, K4) 5 times.

12th row: P30 (K2, P4) twice, K10.

Rep these 12 rows 14 times more. Cast off in patt.

TO MAKE UP

Sew two straight edges tog to form circle. Catch sts at centre, draw up tightly and securely fasten off. Using 3 other colours, make Pompom 5 cm (2 in) in diameter. Attach to top. Turn half g st section to inside and loosely slipstitch into place, encasing elastic circle.

FRED THE DOG

BODY

Beg at rear end

With A, make 4 ch, sl st to form circle.

1st rnd: 1 ch, 2 dc in each of 4 ch, sl st to 1st dc.

2nd rnd: 1 ch, 2 dc in each of 8 dc, sl st to 1st dc.

3rd rnd: 1 ch, 1 dc in 1st dc, (2 dc in next dc, 1 dc in next dc) 7 times, 2 dc in last dc, sl st to 1st dc. 24 dc.

4th rnd: 1 ch, 1 dc in each dc to end, sl st to 1st dc.

5th rnd: 1 ch, 1 dc in each dc to end AT SAME TIME evenly inc 12 dc on rnd, sl st to 1st dc.

6th to 9th rnds: Rep 4th and 5th rnds twice. 60 dc.

Cont in rnds of dc without further inc in

stripes of 4 rnds more in A, 4 rnds in B, 2 rnds in C, 6 rnds in D, 1 rnd in E, 3 rnds in F, 1 rnd in E, 3 rnds in G, 2 rnds in C, 3 rnds in H, 6 rnds in I, 4 rnds in D, 2 rnds in B, 3 rnds in F, 2 rnds in E, 2 rnds in I.

Next rnd: With I, 3 ch, 1 tr in each dc to end, sl st to top of 3 ch.

Next rnd: With I, 1 ch, (insert hook in right side of next st, pass behind it, pushing up left side of same st to front of Work. Work 1 dc around stem of st) rep to end, sl st to first st, break off.

Next rnd: Join B to first st of last rnd, 1 ch, 1 dc in each st of last rnd, sl st to 1st dc. Cont in rnds of dc in stripes of 2 rnds more in B, 2 rnds in A, fasten off. Turn these last 5 rnds to outside, join dark brown to first ch behind these 5 rnds, 3 ch, 1 tr in each ch to end, sl st to top of 3 ch.

Cont in rnds of dc in spiral without working joining sl st until there are 33 rnds of dc in dark brown. Place marker in next dc to denote beg of rnd. Working in rnds of dc as before, evenly dec 12 dc on next and every foll 2nd rnd until 24 dc rem, then work 1 rnd without dec.

Fill Body, then cont in dc rnds as before and evenly dec 12 dc on next rnd, 6 dc on next rnd. Break off, keeping a length of yarn. Thread end of yarn through each of rem 6 dc, pull up and fasten off securely.

HEAD

With dark brown, make 13 ch.

1st rnd: 1 dc in 2nd ch from hook, 1 dc in each of next 10 ch, 5 dc in last ch, working on other side of foundation ch 1 dc in each of next 10 ch, 4 dc in same ch as 1st dc, sl st to 1st dc. 30 dc.

2nd rnd: 1 ch, 2 dc in same place as sl st, 1 dc in each of next 10 dc, 2 dc in each of next 5 dc around curve, 1 dc in each of next 10 dc, 2 dc in each of last 4 dc, sl st to 1st dc. 40 dc.

Cont in rnds of dc, evenly inc 10 dc on every foll 2nd rnd twice. 60 dc. Cont on these 60 dc without further inc for 14 rnds in spiral without working a joining sl st, evenly dec 10 dc on next and foll 4th rnd once more. 40 dc.

Work 3 rnds straight on rem 40 dc. Place marker over 10 dc around each curve, dec 5 dc over marked 10 dc at each curve.

Work 1 rnd without further dec, fasten off. Fill Head and close opening.

HINDLEGS

Beg at Toe , with dark brown, make 4 ch, sl st to form circle, 1 ch, 6 dc in circle. Cont in rnds of dc and evenly inc 6 dc on next 2

rnds. 18 dc *. Work 12 rnds without inc.

**Next rnd: 1 ch, 1 dc in each of 1st 14 dc, TURN.

Working in rows, work 5 more rows dc. Break off, keeping a length of yarn. Fold these 14 dc at top in half and with end of yarn sew dcs tog to form heel.

Rejoin dark brown at top of heel seam, 1 ch, evenly work 18 dc around opening, sl st to 1st dc. Work 4 rnds more in dc, fasten off. Make another one the same. ******

FORELEGS

Work as for Hindlegs to *, then work 4 rnds of dc without inc instead of 12 rnds, then work from ** to ** as for Hindlegs.

TAIL

With dark brown, make 4 ch, sl st to 1st dc to form circle, 1 ch, 6 dc in circle, sl st to 1st dc. Cont in rnds of dc. Work 2 rnds, then

---

MATERIALS

Yarn: 8 ply pure new wool 50 g (2 oz) balls: 3 balls dark brown; scraps of 9 other colours (A, B, C, D, E, F, G, H, I); $1/2$ ball light brown

Notions: One 3.50 ($3^{1}/2$) mm (No. 9) crochet hook; polyester fibre for filling; 2 flat buttons for eyes; 1 round button for nose; strong cotton for joining parts

MEASUREMENTS

43 cm (17 in) long and 23 cm (9 in) high

---

evenly inc 3 dc on next and every foll 4th rnd until there are 18 dc. Work 4 rnds straight, fasten off. With wool sewing needle, thread strong cotton along one side of Tail and pull up to curl slightly.

TONGUE

With red, make 5 ch, 1 dc in 2nd ch from hook, 1 dc in each of next 2 ch, 5 dc in last dc, working on other side of foundation ch work 1 dc in each of next 3 ch, TURN.

Next row: 1 ch, 1 dc in each of 1st 4 dc, 2 dc in next 4 dc, 1 dc in next dc, 2 dc in next dc, 1 dc in each of last 4 dc, fasten off.

MUZZLE

With light brown, make 4 ch, sl st to 1st ch to form circle, 1 ch, 6 dc in circle, sl st to 1st dc. Cont in rnds of dc and evenly inc 6 dc on every rnd until 36 dc, then work 1 rnd without inc, fasten off. Make another one the same. Join 2 cups tog by 4 dc. With black yarn stitch 5 French knots on each

cup. Attach Tongue to inside of cup at joining seam, attach Muzzle with Tongue to lower part of Head, filling cups when they are half attached.

EARS

With light brown, make 13 ch.

1st rnd: 1 dc in 2nd ch from hook, 1 dc in each of next 10 ch, 5 dc in next ch, working on other side of foundation ch work 1 dc in each of next 10 ch, 4 dc in same place as 1st dc, sl st to 1st dc. 30 dc.

2nd rnd: 1 ch, 1 dc in each of 1st 12 dc, * 2 dc in next dc, 1 dc in next dc, 2 dc in next dc *, 1 dc in each of next 12 dc, rep from * to *, sl st to 1st dc.

3rd rnd: 1 ch, 1 dc in each of next 14 dc, * 2 dc in next dc, 1 dc in next dc, 2 dc in next dc *, 1 dc in each of next 14 dc, rep from * to *, sl st to 1st dc. 38 dc.

4th rnd: 1 ch, 1 dc in each of 1st 10 dc, 1 h tr in each of next 2 dc, 2 h tr in each of next 2 dc, 2 tr in each of next 4 dc, 2 h tr in each of next 2 dc, 1 h tr in each of next 2 dc, 1 dc in each of next 12 dc, (2 dc in next dc, 1 dc in next dc) twice. 48 dc.

5th rnd: 1 ch, 1 dc in each of 1st 8 dc, 1 h tr in each of next 4 sts, 1 tr in each of next 5 sts, 2 tr in each of next 6 sts, 1 tr in each of next 5 sts, 1 h tr in each of next 4 sts, 1 dc in each of next 10 dc, (1 dc in next dc, 2 dc in next dc, 1 dc in next dc) twice, sl st to 1st dc, fasten off.

TO MAKE UP

Sew on buttons for eyes and nose, then attach Ears to top of Head. Securely attach Head to front part of Body. Fill Tail, Forelegs and Hindlegs and securely attach them in place.

This Little Pig

Was this the little piggy who went to market? Perhaps that's where he bought these lovely balloons he's carrying home for his little brother who missed all the fun. What a nice thought!

PIGLET JUMPER

BACK

With 3.00 mm (No. 11) needles and A, cast on 81 (87, 93, 101) sts. Work in K1, P1 rib for 5 cm (2 in), ending with WS row. Change to 3.75 mm (No. 9) needles and st st *. Work 2 (6, 12, 20) rows, working from Graph until 90 (100, 114, 130) rows have been worked.

Shape shoulders

Cont to work from Graph, cast/bind off 6 (7, 7, 8) sts at beg of next 2 rows. 69 (73, 79, 85) sts.

Next row: Cast/bind off 7 (7, 8, 8) sts, knit until there are 17 (18, 19, 21) sts on right hand needle, TURN.

Cont on these 17 (18, 19, 21) sts. Dec 1 st at neck edge on next 3 rows AT SAME TIME cast/bind off at beg of every 2nd row 7 (7, 8, 9) sts once, 7 (8, 8, 9) sts once. Ret to rem sts, slip centre 21 (23, 25, 27) sts onto stitch holder, rejoin A at neck edge and complete to match other side.

FRONT

Work as for Back to *, then work 3 (7, 13, 21) rows of st st. Work 1st row of Graph on next row to reverse motif. Cont to work from Graph until 74 (82, 96, 110) rows have been worked. Cont to work from Graph.

Shape Neck

Next row: K35 (37, 39, 42) sts, TURN.
Cont on these sts and cast/bind off at neck edge on next and every 2nd row 2 sts 3 times in all, 1 st twice. 27 (29, 31, 34) sts. Cont on these sts, working from Graph until 90 (100, 114, 130) rows have been worked.

KNITTING FROM A GRAPH

Often instructions for knitting a picture are in the form of a graph, where each square represents one stitch. Work knit rows from right to left and purl rows from left to right. Various colours are sometimes indicated by different symbols or coloured squares.

MATERIALS

Yarn: 5 ply pure wool crepe: 3 (3$\frac{1}{2}$, 3$\frac{1}{2}$, 4) balls. 8 m skeins of tapestry wool: 1 skein purple (PP); 4 skeins light pink (LtP); 5 skeins red (R); 2 skeins yellow (Y); 1 skein blue (B); 4 skeins green (G)

Notions: One pair each 3.75 (3$\frac{3}{4}$) mm (No. 9) and 3.00 (3) mm (No. 11) knitting needles; scrap of embroidery cotton in dark pink for face; st holder

MEASUREMENTS

To fit underarm
        51 (56, 61, 66) cm
        20 (22, 24, 26) in
Garment measures
        59 (64, 69, 76) cm
        23 (25, 27, 29) in
Length   30 (33, 37, 41) cm
        11$\frac{3}{4}$ (13, 14$\frac{1}{2}$, 16) in
Sleeve seam 18 (21, 26, 31) cm
        7 (8, 10, 12) in

TENSION

26 sts and 36 rows to 10 cm (4 in) over picture knit, using 3.75 mm (No. 9) needles. It is important to knit a tension square and to work to the stated tension in order to obtain the required measurements. If your square is bigger use finer needles. If your square is smaller use thicker needles.

Shape shoulder

Cast/bind off at beg of next and every foll 2nd row 6 (7, 7, 8) sts once, 7 (7, 8, 8) sts once, 7 (7, 8, 9) sts once, 7 (8, 8, 9) sts once.

Ret to rem sts, slip centre 11 (13, 15, 17) sts onto st holder, rejoin A at neck edge and complete to match other side.

SLEEVES

With 3.00 mm (No. 9) needles and A, cast on 39 (41, 43, 45) sts. Work in K1, P1 rib for 4 cm (1$\frac{1}{2}$ in), ending with RS row.

Inc row: Rib 4 (5, 6, 7) sts, (inc 1 st in next st, rib 5) rep ending with rib 4 (5, 6, 7) sts instead of rib 5. 45 (47, 49, 51) sts.

Change to 3.75 mm (No. 9) needles and st st. Inc 1 st each end of 5th row once, then on every foll 4th row 7 (7, 5, 4) times, then on every foll 6th row 2 (4, 7, 10) times. 65 (71, 75, 81) sts.

Cont straight on these sts until Sleeve meas 18 (21, 26, 31) cm [7 (8, 10, 12) in]

or length required, ending with WS row. Cast/bind off.

TAIL

With 3.75 mm (No. 9) needles and LtP, cast on 15 sts. Knit 1 row, then purl 1 row. Cast/bind off.

TO MAKE UP

Sew in all ends. Lightly press on wrong side. Coil Tail and lightly press. Embroider face with embroidery thread, and butterflies with contrasting wool, as shown on Graph. Using Swiss darning (knitting stitch) embroider small flowers over Sleeves and lower part of Back and Front. Embroider eyes, buttons and front of piglet's jacket as on Graph. Sew right shoulder seam.

NECKBAND

With RSF, 3.00 mm (No. 11) needles and 5 ply wool in A, pick up and knit 20 (22, 22, 24) sts on left side front neck, knit sts from st holder and evenly inc 3 sts at centre front, knit 20 (22, 22, 24) sts on right side front neck, 4 sts (all sizes) at side back neck, knit and evenly inc 4 sts from st holder at centre back, 4 sts on side neck. 87 (95, 99, 107) sts. Work in K1, P1 rib for 5 cm (2 in). Loosely cast/bind off in rib.

TO FINISH OFF

Sew left shoulder and Neckband. Fold half Neckband to inside and loosely slipstitch in place. Place centre of Sleeve to shoulder seam and sew in Sleeves. Sew side and Sleeve seams. Securely attach Tail.

KEY		----- Stem stitch
▨ PP		∞∞ Chain stitch
☐ LtP		☐ Y
▨ R		▨ B
☒ Button		☐ G
———		66 cm necklines
———		61 cm necklines
———		56 cm necklines
··········		51 cm necklines

Graph for
Flower

Do not work the face or jacket detail on Back.
Reverse the motif for the Front by working the first row as a purl row.

PETAL THE PIGLET

MATERIALS

Yarn: 8 ply pure new wool 50 g (2 oz) balls: 2 balls pink and a small quantity white; 5 ply pure new wool: small quantity in 3 other colours
Notions: One each 3.50 (3½) mm (No. 9) and 3.00 (3) mm (No. 11) crochet hooks; polyester fibre for filling; two small buttons for eyes

MEASUREMENTS

21 cm (8 in) long

BODY

Make 2

Beg at top edge and work in dc. With 3.50 mm (No. 9) hook and pink yarn, make 23 ch.

1st row: 1 dc in 2nd ch from hook, 1 dc in each ch to end. 22 dc.

2nd to 4th rows: 2 ch, 1 dc in 2nd ch from hook, 1 dc in each dc to last dc, 2 dc in last dc. 1 dc at each end has been inc.

5th row: 3 ch (front), 1 dc in 2nd ch from hook, 1 dc in next ch, then in each dc to last dc, 2 dc in last dc.

6th row: Work as 2nd row.

Rep last 2 rows twice more. 43 dc. Inc 1 dc

at each end as before on next and foll 2nd row once more. 47 dc. Work 1 row without inc, ending at front edge.

Shape jaw

Dec 1 dc at front edge only on every row until 41 dc rem. Cont to dec 1 dc at front edge as before AT SAME TIME dec 1 dc at back edge on next and foll 4th row once more, ending at back edge. 34 dc.

Shape hindleg

*Next row: 1 ch, 1 dc in each of 1st 13 dc, TURN.

Dec 1 dc at inner edge on every row AT SAME TIME dec 1 dc at back edge on foll 4th row from last dec. 9 dc.

Work 2 rows without dec, fasten off.

Shape foreleg

Next row: Rejoin pink to 9th dc from hindleg, 1 ch 1 dc in same dc as join, 1 dc in each dc to end. 13 dc.

Dec 1 dc at front edge on next row then work straight AT SAME TIME dec 1 dc at inner edge on every row until 8 dc rem.

Work 1 row without dec, fasten off *.

UNDERBODY

Make 2

With 3.50 mm (No. 9) hook and pink yarn, make 38 ch and work in dc. Work 1 row, then dec 1 dc at beg (front edge) of next row. Cont to dec 1 dc at front edge on next 2 rows, ending at back edge. 34 dc.

Work from * to * of Body. Securely join two pieces tog along foundation chs.

TOP GUSSET

Beg at back end, using a 3.50 mm (No. 9) hook and pink yarn, make 2 ch, 1 dc in 2nd

ch from hook.

Next row: 2 ch, 1 dc in 2nd ch from hook, 1 dc in next dc.

Next row: 2 ch, 1 dc in 2nd ch from hook, 1 dc in each dc to end.

Rep last row until there are 9 dc. Work further 37 rows without inc, then dec 1 dc at beg of next and every foll 5th row until 4 dc rem, then on every foll 3rd row until 1 dc rem, fasten off.

EARS

Make 2

With 3.50 mm (No. 9) hook and pink, make 3 ch, 1 dc in 2nd ch from hook, 1 dc in next ch. 2 dc.

Cont in dc and inc 1 dc at beg of next 6 rows. 8 dc.

Work 1 row without inc, then cont to work in dc around 2 sides of triangle, fasten off.

TAIL

With 3.50 mm (No. 9) hook and pink, make 11 ch, 2 dc in 2nd ch from hook, 2 dc in each ch to end. Work 1 row of dc without inc, fasten off.

NOSE

With 3.50 mm (No. 9) hook and white, make 5 ch, 1 dc in 2nd ch from hook, 1 dc in each of next 2 ch, 4 dc in last ch, working on other side of foundation ch, work 1 dc in each of next 2 ch, 3 dc in same place as 1st dc, sl st to 1st dc.

Next rnd: 1 ch, 1 dc in each of 1st 4 dc, 2 dc in each of next 3 dc, 1 dc in each of next 3 dc, 2 dc in each of next 2 dc, 1 dc in same place as 1st dc, sl st to 1st dc. Fasten off.

FLOWERS

With 3.00 mm (No. 11) hook and 5 ply yarn, make 5 ch, sl st to 1st ch to form circle, (3 ch, 2 tr, 3 ch, sl st) 3 or 4 times in circle. Fasten off. Using 3 different colours make as many Flowers as desired.

TO MAKE UP

Neatly join Underbody to each Body piece around legs, then to front and back edges over 10 rows. Matching point of long, shaped end of Gusset to front end of Underbody, smoothly join Gusset around front edge, then top edge of Body, ending halfway down back edge, leaving 5 cm (2 in) opening on one side. Fill firmly, rearranging filling with point of needle for better shaping. Close opening. Securely attach Ears, Tail, Nose and Eyes. Embroider nostrils and sew crochet Flowers all over Body as shown. For very young children, embroider the eyes.

KAMAHL ELEPHANT

TRUNK
Make 2

With grey, make 5 ch, 1 dc in 2nd ch from hook, 1 dc in each of next 3 ch. 4 dc. Cont in dc. Work until there are 7 rows from beg, then inc 1 dc at beg of next and foll 4th row once, then inc 1 dc at same edge on next 3 rows. 9 dc. Fasten off.

* FIRST LEG
With grey, make 13 ch, 1 dc in 2nd ch from hook, 1 dc in each ch to end. 12 dc. Cont in dc. Work 5 rows more straight, inc 1 dc at beg of next row, then on every foll 2nd row twice more. 15 dc. Fasten off.

Make 2nd leg the same. Do not fasten off.

Shape body
1st row: 1 ch, 1 dc in each of 15 dc, make 7 ch, beginning at shaped edge, work 1 dc in each of 15 dc on other leg.

2nd row: 1 ch, 2 dc in 1st dc, 1 dc in each dc and ch to last dc, 2 dc in last dc. 39 dc. Place marker in last dc for front edge.

Inc 1 dc at front edge on every foll 2nd row 3 times more, AT SAME TIME inc 1 dc at back edge on foll 4th row from last inc, then work 2 rows without inc. 43 dc.*

Next row: 4 ch, 1 dc in 2nd ch from hook, 1 dc in each ch and dc to end.

Next row: 1 ch, 2 dc in 1st dc, 1 dc in each dc to end of Body, beg at shaped edge work 1 dc in each of 9 dc over Trunk. 56 dc. Work 1 row, inc 1 dc at front edge on next row, then on every foll 4th row twice. 59 dc. Dec 1 dc at back edge on next and foll 2nd row once more. 57 dc rem.

Next row: 1 ch, miss 1st dc, 1 dc in 2nd and in each dc to end.

Rep last row twice more, 54 dc rem, ending at front edge.

MATERIALS
Yarn: 8 ply pure wool 50 g (2 oz) balls: 3 balls grey; 5 ply pure wool: small quantity each of pink, gold and black

Notions: One 3.50 (3$^{1}/_{2}$) mm (No. 9) crochet hook; polyester fibre for filling; 2 buttons for eyes.

MEASUREMENT
18 cm (7 in) high

Shape head
1st row: 1 ch, miss 1st dc, 1 dc in 2nd and in each dc until 31 dc have been made, TURN

2nd row: Sl st in 2nd dc, 1 dc in next and in each dc to last 2 dc, dec 1 dc.

3rd row: 1 ch, miss 1st dc, 1 dc in 2nd and in each dc to last 2 dc, TURN

Rep last 2 rows 3 times more. 7 dc rem. Fasten off.

Make other half the same.

UNDERBODY
Make 2

Work from * to *, fasten off.

HEAD GUSSET
With grey, make 2 ch, 2 dc in 1st ch. Cont in dc and inc 1 dc in 1st dc on every row until 10 dc rem, then work 14 rows straight on these 10 dc. Dec 1 dc at beg of next and every row until 1 dc rem. Fasten off.

EARS
Make 2

With grey, make 14 ch, 1 tr in 4th ch from hook, 1 tr in each ch to last ch, 2 tr in last ch. 13 tr, counting 3 ch as 1 tr.

Next row: 3 ch, 1 tr in 1st tr, 1 tr in each tr to 3 ch at end, 2 tr in top of 3 ch.

Rep last row twice more. 19 tr. Cont in tr and work 7 rows straight on these 19 tr, dec 1 tr at each end of next 4 rows. 11 tr rem. Fasten off.

RUG
With 5 ply pink, make 17 ch, 1 tr in 4th ch from hook, 1 tr in each ch to end. 15 tr, counting 3 ch as 1 tr.

Cont in tr and work until there are 16 rows from beg, then cont to work around all edges as follows: 1 ch, smoothly work in dc along side edge, 3 dc in next corner, 1 dc in each foundation ch to next corner, 3 dc in corner, smoothly work in dc along side edge to top edge, 3 dc in corner, 1 dc in each tr along top edge, 3 dc in corner, sl st to 1st dc. Break off.

With RS facing, join gold to centre dc at corner, 3 ch, 2 tr in same place as join, *3 ch, sl st to top of last tr, 1 tr in each of next 3 dc, rep from * to end AT SAME TIME work 5 tr in centre dc at each of 4 corners. Sl st to top of 3 ch. Fasten off.

TO MAKE UP
Using small backstitch, and leaving centre 6.5 cm (2$^{1}/_{2}$ in) open, join Underbody pieces tog, then neatly join to Body around all edges. Beg at top end of Trunk, neatly sew Head Gusset along front edge of head sections. Turn work right side out and fill firmly, arranging filling with point of needle for better shape. Fold each Ear in half across width and sew each side edge, leaving top end open. Turn right side out. Attach to sides of head. Sew on buttons for eyes. Attach Rug to centre back. With 5 ply black, stitch hooves. With grey, used double, make 6 cm (2$^{1}/_{4}$ in) long cord with a tassel on one end then attach to end of Body.

HINT
Knitted and crochet toys are a great favourite with young children, but remember if you are making one for a child under three years of age you should embroider the eyes and not use buttons. Very young children can remove buttons and beads and can choke on them quite easily.

Polyester fibre is ideal for stuffing toys as it is very soft, unlikely to cause allergy problems and can be washed if you need to.

Smart Set

Too young for college but never too young for a smart college look. Dressed in cables and smart crochet, this pair are definitely dressed for success!

CABLE SUIT

JUMPER
BACK
With 3.25 mm (No. 10) needles, cast on 67 (73, 77) sts. Knit 12 rows*. Change to 4.00 mm (No. 8) needles and st st.
Work until piece meas 19 (20.5, 23) cm [7$\frac{1}{2}$ (8, 9) in] from beg, ending with WS row. Adjust length at this point if required, ending with WS row.
Shape raglans
Cast/bind off 3 sts (all sizes) at beg of next 2 rows. Dec 1 st each end of every row 5 times, then on every foll 2nd row until 25 (27, 27) sts rem.
Work 1 row. Leave sts on st holder.
POCKET LININGS
Make 2
With 4.00 mm (No. 8) needles, cast on 20 (22, 24) sts and work in st st for 24 rows.
Leave sts on spare needle.
FRONT
Work as Back to *. Change to 4.00 mm (No. 8) needles and cont as follows:
1st row: K15 (16, 17) sts, inc 1 st in each of next 4 sts, K29 (33, 35) sts, inc 1 st in each of next 4 sts, K15 (16, 17) sts. 75 (81, 85) sts.
2nd row: P15 (16, 17) sts, K2, P4, K2, P29 (33, 35) sts, K2, P4, K2, P15 (16, 17) sts.
3rd row: K15 (16, 17) sts, P2, K4, P2, K29 (33, 35) sts, P2, K4, P2, K15 (16, 17) sts.
4th row: As 2nd row.
5th row: K15 (16, 17) sts, P2, C4, P2, K29

(33, 35) sts, P2, C4, P2, K15 (16, 17) sts.
Rep from 2nd to 5th rows inclusive 4 times, then 2nd and 3rd rows once more.
24th row: P15 (16, 17) sts, *K2 tog, (P2 tog) twice, K2 tog*, P29 (33, 35) sts, rep from * to * once, P15 (16, 17) sts. 67 (73, 77) sts.
25th row: K7, *place Pocket Lining at back of work, knit next st tog with first st of Pocket Lining, slip next 18 (20, 22) sts of main section onto st holder, K18 (20, 22)

MATERIALS
Yarn: For Jumper: 8 ply pure wool 50 g (2 oz) balls: 3$\frac{1}{2}$ (4, 4$\frac{1}{2}$) balls
For Slacks: same as for Jumper
Notions: One pair each 4.00 (4) mm (No. 8) and 3.25 (3$\frac{1}{4}$) mm (No. 10) knitting needles; cable needle; set of four 3.25 (3$\frac{1}{4}$) mm (No. 10) knitting needles and stitch holders for Jumper; elastic for Slacks

MEASUREMENTS
To fit underarm 51 (56, 61) cm
    20 (22, 24) in
Garment measures
    56 (61, 66) cm
    22 (24, 26) in
Length of Jumper
    30 (33, 37) cm
    11$\frac{3}{4}$ (13, 14$\frac{1}{2}$)
Sleeve seam 20 (23, 28) cm
    8 (9, 11) in
Slacks width at hips
    56 (61, 66) cm
    22 (24, 26) in
Outside leg length
    47 (52, 61) cm
    18$\frac{1}{2}$ (20$\frac{1}{2}$, 24$\frac{1}{2}$) in

TENSION
23 sts and 32 rows to 10 cm (4 in) over st st, using 4.00 mm (No. 8) needles.
It is important to knit a tension square and to work to the stated tension in order to obtain the required measurements. If your square is bigger use finer needles. If your square is smaller use thicker needles.

SPECIAL ABBREVIATION
C4 = Cable 4 stitches: slip next 2 sts onto cable needle and hold at back of work, K2, then K2 from cable needle

---

sts over Pocket Lining, knit next st tog with last st of lining*, K13 (15, 15) sts, rep from * to * once, K7.
26th row: Purl to end.
Cont in st st until piece meas same as Back to raglan shaping, ending with WS row.
Shape raglans
Work as for Back until 43 (45, 45) sts rem, ending with RS row.
Shape neck
1st row: P17 sts (all sizes), TURN.
Cont on these 17 sts, dec 1 st at neck edge on every row 3 times, then on every foll 2nd row 3 times AT SAME TIME dec 1 st at raglan edge on every foll 2nd row as before until 2 sts rem.
Work 2 sts tog, fasten off.
Ret to rem sts, leave centre 9 (11, 11) sts on st holder, rejoin yarn at neck edge and complete to match other side.
POCKET BORDERS
With RS facing, 3.25 mm (No. 10) needles, rejoin yarn and knit 6 rows. Cast/bind off. Neatly attach Pocket Linings, then ends of Borders.
SLEEVES
With 3.25 mm (No. 10) needles, cast on 34 (36, 38) sts. Knit 12 rows. Change to 4.00 mm (No. 8) needles and cont as follows:
1st row: K15 (16, 17) sts, inc 1 st in each of next 4 sts, K15 (16, 17) sts. 38 (40, 42) sts.
2nd row: P15 (16, 17) sts, K2, P4, K2, P15 (16, 17) sts.
3rd row: K15 (16, 17) sts, P2, K4, P2, knit to end.
4th row: As 2nd row.
5th row: K15 (16, 17) sts, P2, C4, P2, knit to end.
Rep last 4 rows for C4 patt AT SAME TIME inc 1 st each end of 7th row once, then on every foll 8th row until there are 50 (54, 58) sts, taking all inc sts into st st.
Cont without further inc until sleeve meas 20 (23, 28) cm [8 (9, 11) in] ending with WS row. Adjust length at this point if required ending with WS row.
Shape raglans
Cont to work C4 patt at centre as before, cast/bind off 3 sts (all sizes) at beg of next 2 rows, then dec 1 st each end of next and every foll 2nd row until 12 sts rem for all sizes.
Work 1 row. Leave sts on st holder.

TO MAKE UP
Press on wrong side, except for cables.

HINT

Before you assemble a knitted garment it is usual to press the pieces lightly on the wrong side following the instructions on the ball band of the yarn. Patterns, ribbing and cables are very rarely pressed, in order to retain their shape and elasticity. Some pieces, particularly the very textured patterns, can be blocked to achieve correct shape (see page 4).

Sew four raglan seams, then sew side and sleeve seams.

NECKBAND

With RS facing, a set of four 3.25 mm (No. 10) needles, beg at left back raglan seam, *K2, K2 tog, K4, K2 tog, K2* over Left Sleeve, pick up and knit 16 sts (all sizes) on each side of front neck, K9 (11, 11) sts at centre front neck, rep from * to * over Right Sleeve, K25 (27, 27) sts on back neck. 86 (90, 90) sts.

Work in rnds of K1, P1 rib for 6 cm (2½ in). Cast/bind off loosely in rib.

Fold half Neckband to inside and loosely stitch in place.

SLACKS

RIGHT LEG

Beg at waist, with 3.25 mm (No. 10) needles, loosely cast on 62 (68, 74) sts. Work 8 rows st st. Purl 1 row for hemline. Change to 4.00 mm (No. 8) needles. Beg with purl row cont in st st until work is 3 cm (1¼ in) from hemline*, ending with WS row.

Shape back

Next 2 rows: K7 (8, 9) sts, TURN, sl1, purl to end.

Next 2 rows: K14 (16, 18) sts, TURN, sl1, purl to end.

Cont to shape in this way working 7 (8, 9) sts more each time until 28 (32, 36) sts have been worked, TURN, sl1, purl to end. Cont in C4 patt as follows:

1st row: K29 (32, 35), inc 1 st in each of next 4 sts, K14 (15, 16), sl1 knitwise (front crease), K14 (16, 18) sts. 66 (72, 78) sts.

2nd row: P14 (16, 18) sts, yrn, P1 (for front crease), P14 (15, 16) sts, K2, P4, K2, P29 (32, 35) sts.

3rd row: K29 (32, 35) sts, P2, K4, P2, K14 (15, 16) sts, sl1 knitwise and drop next loop made by yrn, K14 (16, 18) sts.

4th row: As 2nd row.

5th row: K29 (32, 35) sts, P2, C4, P2, K14 (15, 16) sts, sl1 knitwise and drop next loop made by yrn, K14 (16, 18) sts.

Rep from 2nd to 5th rows inclusive for C4 patt and front crease.

**Cont in patt until the work meas 11 (12, 13) cm [4½ (4¾, 5) in] from hemline at front edge ending with WS row.

Keeping patt correct cont as follows:

Shape crotch

Inc 1 st each end of next row, then on every foll 6th row twice, then on foll 4th row once, on every foll 2nd row 3 times. 80 (86,

92) sts. Work 1 row**.

Cast on 2 (3, 4) sts at beg of next row for Back, then 2 sts (all sizes) at beg of next row for Front. 84 (91, 98) sts.

***Place marker at centre of last row.

Shape leg

Dec 1 st each end of next row, then on every foll 2nd row 3 times more, on foll 4th row twice, on foll 6th row once, then on foll 8th row once. 68 (75, 82) sts rem.

Cont straight on these rem sts until work meas 25 (29, 37) cm [9¾ (11½, 14½) in] from marker ending with WS row. Adjust length at this point if required, ending with WS row.

Change to 3.25 mm (No. 10) needles and knit 12 rows. Cast/bind off.

LEFT LEG

Work as Right Leg to *, ending with RS row.

Shape back

Next 2 rows: P7 (8, 9) sts, TURN sl1, knit to end.

Next 2 rows: P14 (8, 9) sts, TURN sl1, knit to end.

Cont to shape in this way working 7 (8, 9)

sts more each time until 28 (32, 36) sts have been worked, TURN, sl1, knit to end. Purl 1 row over all sts.

Cont in C4 patt as follows:

1st row: K14 (16, 18) sts, sl1 knitwise (for front crease), K14 (15, 16) sts, inc 1 st in each of next 4 sts, K29 (32, 35) sts. 66 (72, 78) sts.

2nd row: P29 (32, 35) sts, K2, P4, K2, P14 (15, 16) sts, yrn, P1 (for front crease), P14 (16, 18) sts.

Cont to work C4 patt and front crease line as set. Work from ** to ** of Right Leg.

Keeping C4 patt and front crease correct cont as follows:

Shape crotch

Cast on 2 sts (all sizes) at beg of next row, then 2 (3, 4) sts at beg of next row. 84 (91, 98) sts.

Work as Right Leg from *** to end.

TO MAKE UP

Press on wrong side, except cables. Sew up centre back and front seams, then inside Leg seams. Cut elastic to waist size and join ends to form a circle, place inside waist. Catch sts loosely over elastic.

63

CROCHET JACKET

MATERIALS
Yarn: 5 ply pure wool crepe 50 g (2 oz) balls: 5 (6, 6, 7) balls navy (A); 1 ball (all sizes) grey (B); small quantity Second Contrast mauve (C)
Notions: One each of 3.50 ($3^1/2$) mm (No. 9) and 3.00 (3) mm (No. 11) crochet hooks, 5 buttons

MEASUREMENTS
To fit underarm
          51 (56, 61, 66) cm
          20 (22, 24, 26) in
Garment measures
          56 (61, 66, 71) cm
          22 (24, 26, 28) in
Length   30 (33, 37, 41) cm
          $11^3/4$ (13, $14^1/2$, 16) in
Sleeve seam 20 (24, 29, 33) cm
          8 ($9^1/2$, $11^1/4$, 13) in

TENSION
17 tr to 8 cm ($3^1/8$ in) and 8 rows of tr to 7 cm ($2^3/4$ in) using 3.50 mm (No. 9) hook. It is important to knit a tension square and to work to the stated tension in order to obtain the required measurements. If your square is bigger use finer needles. If your square is smaller use thicker needles.

SPECIAL ABBREVIATION
Dec 1 tr = decrease 1 treble: (yoh, insert hook in next tr, yoh and draw through loop, yoh and draw through 2 loops on hook) twice, yoh and draw through 3 loops on hook

NOTE
Always work sl st in 1st tr, pull yarn slightly to tighten loop of sl st, work 3 ch (counts as 1 tr), and always work last tr on next row in top of this 3 ch

BACK
With 3.50 mm (No. 9) hook and A, make 62 (68, 72, 78) ch.
1st row: (WS) sl st in 2nd ch from hook, 3 ch, 1 tr in each ch to end of row. 61 (67, 71, 77) tr.

2nd row: Sl st in 1st tr, 3 ch, 1 tr in each tr to end, working last tr in top of 3 ch.
Rep last row until there are 23 (25, 27, 31) rows from beg, ending with WS row. Adjust length at this point if required, ending with WS row.
Shape armholes
1st row: Sl st in each of 1st 4 (5, 4, 5) tr, 1 dc in next tr, 1 h tr in next tr, 1 tr in each tr to last 6 (7, 6, 7) tr, 1 h tr in next tr, 1 dc in next tr, sl st in next tr, TURN.
2nd row: Sl st in each of 1 dc, 1 h tr and 1 tr, 3 ch, dec 1 tr, 1 tr in each tr to last 3 tr, dec 1 tr, 1 tr in last tr, TURN.
3rd row: Sl st in 1st tr, 3 ch, dec 1 tr, 1 tr in each tr to last 3 tr, dec 1 tr, 1 tr in last tr. Rep last row 1 (1, 2, 2) times more. Cont straight on rem 43 (47, 51, 55) tr until there are 11 (12, 15, 16) rows of tr in armholes, ending with RS (WS, RS, WS) row.
Shape shoulders and neck
1st row: Sl st in 1st tr, 1 dc in each of next 1 (1, 2, 2) tr, 1 h tr in each of next 1 (1, 2, 2) tr, 1 tr in each of next 11 (12, 12, 13) tr, 1 h tr in next tr, 1 dc in next tr, sl st in next tr, fasten off, TURN.
2nd row: Miss 1 dc and 1 h tr, rejoin A to 1st tr, 3 ch, dec 1 tr, 1 tr in each of next 1 (2, 1, 2) tr, 1 h tr in each of next 1 (1, 2, 2) tr, 1 dc in each of 1 (1, 2, 2) tr, sl st in next tr, fasten off.
Miss centre 9 (11, 11, 13) tr, rejoin A to next tr, and cont for other side as follows:
1st row: 1 dc in next tr, 1 h tr in next tr, 1 tr in each of next 11 (12, 12, 13) tr, 1 h tr in each of next 1 (1, 2, 2) tr, 1 dc in each of next 1 (1, 2, 2) tr, sl st in last tr, fasten off, TURN.
2nd row: Rejoin A to 7th (8th, 9th, 10th) tr from neck edge, 1 dc in each of next 1 (1, 2, 2) tr, 1 h tr in each of next 1 (1, 2, 2) tr, 1 tr in each of next 1 (2, 1, 2) tr, dec 1 tr, 1 tr in last tr, fasten off.
POCKET LININGS
Make 2
With 3.50 mm (No. 9) hook and A, make 21 (22, 24, 25) ch and work in tr as for Back. 20 (21, 23, 24) tr for 7 (8, 9, 10) rows, fasten off.
RIGHT FRONT
With 3.50 mm (No. 9) hook and A, make 33 (36, 38, 41) ch and work in tr as before. There should be 32 (35, 37, 40) tr in a row. Cont in tr until there are 9 (11, 11, 13) rows from beg, ending with WS row.
Make pocket opening
1st row: Sl st in 1st tr, 3 ch, 1 tr in each of next 9 (11, 11, 12) tr, place Pocket Lining

at back of work, inserting hook through next tr and 1st tr of Lining work 1 tr, 1 tr in each of next 18 (19, 21, 22) tr over Lining, miss 18 (19, 21, 22) tr of Front, inserting hook through next tr and last tr of Lining work 1 tr, 1 tr in each of last 2 (2, 2, 3) tr of Front. Cont in tr as before until work measures same as Back to armhole, ending with WS row.
Shape armhole and neck
1st row: Sl st in 1st tr, 3 ch, dec 1 tr, 1 tr in each tr to last 8 (9, 8, 9) tr, 1 h tr in next tr, 1 dc in next tr, sl st in next tr, TURN.
2nd row: Sl st in each of 1 dc, 1 h tr and 1 tr, 3 ch, dec 1 tr, 1 tr in each tr to last 3 tr, dec 1 tr, 1 tr in last tr.
Cont to dec 1 tr each end as before on next 2 (2, 3, 3) rows, then cont straight at armhole edge and dec 1 tr at front edge only on next 4 (5, 4, 5) rows. Cont on rem 13 (14, 16, 17) tr until there are 11 (12, 15, 16) rows of tr in armhole, ending with RS (WS, RS, WS) row.
Shape shoulder
1st and 3rd sizes only
1st row: Sl st in 1st tr, 1 dc in each of next 1 (2) tr, 1 h tr in each of next 1 (2) tr, 1 tr in each of next 10 (11) tr.
2nd row: Sl st in 1st tr, 3 ch, 1 tr in each of next 2 (3) tr, 1 h tr in each of next 1 (2) tr, 1 dc in each of next 1 (2) tr, sl st in next tr, fasten off.
2nd, 4th sizes only
1st row: Sl st in 1st tr, 3 ch, 1 tr in each of next 10 (11) tr, 1 h tr in each of next 1 (2) tr, 1 dc in each of next 1 (2) tr, sl st in next tr, fasten off, TURN.
2nd row: Rejoin A to 8th (10th) tr from neck edge, 1 dc in each of next 1 (2) tr, 1 h tr in each of next 1 (2) tr, 1 tr in each tr to end, fasten off.

HINT

Maintaining correct and even tension is crucial to achieving the right size and texture for your crochet work. It is easiest to do this if you keep moving your left hand, which controls the feeding of the yarn close to the hook after every couple of stitches. Making stitches over the shank of the hook will help to keep them even.

LEFT FRONT

Work as Right Front, reversing pocket position and all shapings.

LEFT SLEEVE

With 3.50 mm (No. 9) hook and A, make 33 (35, 37, 39) ch, then work 2 rows in tr as before – 32 (34, 36, 38) tr, then inc 1 tr each end of next and every foll 3rd row until there are 44 (48, 54, 58) tr, then cont without further inc until sleeve meas 19 (23, 28, 32) cm [7$\frac{1}{2}$ (9, 11, 12$\frac{1}{2}$) in] from beg, ending with WS row. Adjust length at this point if required, ending with WS row.*

Shape top

1st row: Sl st in each of 1st 4 (5, 4, 5) tr, 1 dc in next tr, 1 h tr in next tr, 1 tr in each tr to last 8 (9, 8, 9) tr, 1 h tr in next tr, 1 dc in next tr, sl st in next tr, TURN.

**2nd row: Sl st in each of 1 dc, 1 h tr and 1 tr, 3 ch, dec 1 tr, 1 tr in each tr to last 3 tr, dec 1 tr, 1 tr in last tr.

Cont to dec 1 tr each end of next 5 (6, 7, 8) rows. 18 (18, 24, 24) tr.

Next row: Sl st in 1st tr, 1 dc in next tr, 1 h tr in next tr, 1 tr in each tr to last 3 tr, 1 h tr in next tr, 1 dc in next tr, sl st in last tr.

Next row: Sl st in 1 dc and 1 h tr, then work as last row, fasten off.

RIGHT SLEEVE

Work as Left Sleeve to *

Shape top

Next row: Sl st in each of 1st 6 (7, 6, 7) tr, 1 dc in next tr, 1 h tr in next tr, 1 tr in each tr to last 6 (7, 6, 7) tr, 1 h tr in next tr, 1 dc in next tr, sl st in next tr, TURN.

Finish as Left Sleeve from ** to end.

TO STITCH STRIPES

Sew side seams, and leave shoulders free until all stripes are worked. On Back, with wool sewing needle and C, beg at lower edge of centre tr, insert needle from WS and pull to RS of piece, then passing needle behind st insert needle from right to left of tr, *always facing RS of piece and passing needle behind st, insert needle from right to left of tr above last tr just worked – now contrast colour is worked around stem of tr, rep from * working upward to top, then secure colour on WS cut off. Using B, work same way along trs on both sides of C stripes. Miss 6 tr on right and left sides of these centre 3 stripes, and work B, C and B stripes on next 3 trs. Cont in this way until Back piece is finished, then cont to work on Front pieces. Work stripes on Sleeves in same way.

FRONT AND NECK BORDER

Lightly press on WS. Sew shoulder seams.

With RS facing and 3.00 mm (No. 11) hook, join A to lower edge of Right Front, 1 ch, 2 dc in each of 23 (25, 27, 31) tr rows, or to beg of neck shaping, 3 dc in next tr row and place marker in 1st of these 3 dc to denote beg of neck, 2 dc in each of next 12 (13, 16, 17) tr rows, cont over back neck work 2 dc in next tr row, 2 dc in side of next h tr, 1 dc in next dc, 1 dc in each of centre 9 (11, 11, 13) tr, 1 dc in next dc, 2 dc in side of next h tr, 2 dc in next tr row, cont on left front neck and work 2 dc in each of next 12 (13, 16, 17) tr rows, 3 dc in next tr row and place marker in last dc of these 3 dc to denote beg of neck *3 ch, miss 1 tr row, 2 dc in each of next 4 (4, 5, 6) tr rows, rep from * 3 times more, 3 ch, miss 1 tr row, 2 dc in each of last 2 (4, 2, 2) tr rows, TURN. Adjust buttonhole position if necessary.

Next row: 1 ch, 1 dc in each dc, 2 dc in each of 5 button loops, and 2 dc in the dc at beg of neck shaping, TURN.

Next row: 1 ch, 1 dc in each dc to end, AT SAME TIME 2 dc in dc at beg of neck shaping, then cont to work along lower edge as follows: 3 dc in lower corner, 1 dc

The Rabbit pictured above is knitted following the instructions on page 27

in each foundation ch to end, 3 dc in corner, sl st to next dc, fasten off.

Next row: With RS facing rejoin A to a dc at side seam, 1 ch, working from left to right work 1 dc in each dc along all edges, sl st to first st, fasten off. One round of backward dc has been worked.

POCKET BORDERS

With RS facing, 3.00 mm (No. 11) hook and A, work 3 rows of dc, then work 1 row of backward dc, fasten off.

SLEEVE BORDERS

With RS facing, 3.00 mm (No. 11) hook, join A to seam, 1 ch, 1 dc in each foundation ch to end, sl st to 1st dc, TURN. With WS facing work 1 rnd of dc, then with RS facing work 1 more round of dc, then with RS facing again work 1 rnd of backward dc, fasten off.

TO FINISH OFF

Smoothly fit Sleeves into armholes, then attach Pocket Linings and neatly attach ends of Pocket Borders. Sew on buttons.

Toyland

Dolls for the young armchair traveller from all around the globe –
Edward guards the Tower of London, Rosalita dances the flamenco, Yukio has
a farm on Mt Fuji and Hanna grows Tulips and lives in an old windmill.

HANNA, THE DUTCH DOLL

HEAD AND BODY

With 3.00 mm (No. 11) hook and natural, make 5 ch, sl st to 1st ch to form circle.

1st rnd: Work 1 ch, and 2 dc in each of 5 ch, sl st to 1st dc.

2nd rnd: Work 2 dc in each of 10 dc, sl st to 1st dc.

Work in rnds of dc and evenly inc 10 dc on every foll 2nd rnd until there are 50 dc. Cont 14 rnds more in dc in spiral without working sl st, evenly dec 10 dc on next and every foll 2nd rnd until 20 dc rem. Work 5 rnds on these rem 20 dc, evenly inc 10 dc on next and foll 2nd rnd once more, then on foll 2nd rnd evenly inc 5 dc. 45 dc. Cont to work 26 rnds more in dc in spiral without working sl st, fasten off.

LEGS

Make 2

With 3.00 mm (No. 11) hook and black, make 5 ch, sl st to 1st ch to form circle, 1 ch, 2 dc in each of 5 ch, sl st to 1st dc. Cont in rnds of dc and evenly inc 5 dc on next 2 rnds. 20 dc. Work 5 rnds in dc on these 20 dc, break off. Join natural, cont to work 36 rnds more in dc in spiral, fasten off.

ARMS

Make 2

With 3.00 mm (No. 11) hook and natural, make 5 ch, sl st to 1st ch to form circle, 1 ch, 2 dc in each of 5 ch, sl st to 1st dc. Cont in rnds of dc, evenly inc 5 dc on next rnd. 15 dc.

Cont on these 15 dc for 20 rnds in spiral.

Next rnd: 1 dc in each of 1st 3 dc, 1 h tr in each of next 2 dc, 1 tr in each of next 6 dc, 1 h tr in each of next 2 dc, 1 dc in each of last 2 dc.

Next rnd: 1 dc in each of 15 sts.

Rep last 2 rnds 3 times more, fasten off.

TO MAKE UP

Fill Body, Head, Legs and Arms. Matching dc to dc, join every dc of one Leg to lower end of Body. Catch 2 dc tog at centre of Body for Crotch, then cont to join other Leg as before. Securely attach Arms in place.

DRESS

Worked in tr. With 3.50 mm (No. 9) hook

and black, make 36 ch.

1st row: 1 tr in 4th ch from hook, 1 tr in each ch to end, 34 tr, drop yarn, TURN.

2nd row: Join a contrast colour to 1st tr, 3 ch, 1 tr in next and in each tr to end, fasten off, DO NOT TURN.

MATERIALS

Yarn: 5 ply pure new wool 50 g (2 oz) balls: 1¹⁄₂ balls natural; 1 ball black; small quantity each in 15 other colours for dress; ¹⁄₂ ball dark brown for hair

Notions: One each 3.50 (3¹⁄₂) mm (No. 9) and 3.00 (3) mm (No. 11) crotchet hooks; polyester fibre for filling; two 17 cm (6³⁄₄ in) squares of white cotton fabric for Bonnet; 10 cm x 14 cm (4 in x 5¹⁄₂ in) piece of white cotton fabric for Apron; 90 cm (35¹⁄₂ in) of 1.5 cm (¹⁄₂ in) wide lace for trimming; 46 cm (18 in); 46 cm (18 in) of 16 mm (¹⁄₂ in) wide ribbon; 2 small buttons for Dress; 16.5 cm x 10 cm (6¹⁄₂ in x 4 in) cardboard; thin plastic bag

MEASUREMENT

38 cm (15 in) high

NOTE

(1 dc 2 ch) at beg of tr row stands for 1 tr. Always work last tr of next row into top of (1 dc 2 ch)

3rd row: Ret to beg of last row, insert hook in top of 3 ch and pull through black, 3 ch, 1 tr in next and in each tr to end, drop yarn, TURN.

Using 15 colours and black, rep last 2 rows until there are 46 rows of tr in all, fasten off. Join foundation ch and last row tog, matching each st. Sew in all ends on wrong side of work.

With RS facing, join black to side of a tr row, and cont for bodice as follows:

1st row: 1 ch, 1 dc in same place as join, 1 dc in side of each tr row to end, TURN.

2nd row: 1 ch, 1 dc in 1st and each dc to end, TURN.

3rd row: (1 dc 2 ch) in 1st dc, 1 tr in 2nd and in each dc to end, TURN.

Divide for armholes

1st row: (1 dc 2 ch) in 1st tr, 1 tr in each of next 9 tr, TURN.

Work 3 rows more in tr.

Next row: Sl st in each of 1st 5 tr, (1 dc 2 ch) in next tr, 1 tr in each of last 4 tr, fasten off. Right back is worked.

Miss next 3 tr from right back, join black to next tr, and cont for front as follows:

1st row: (1 dc 2 ch) in same tr as join, 1 tr in each of next 19 tr, TURN.

Cont in tr for 3 more rows.

Next row: (1 dc 2 ch) in 1st tr, 1 tr in each of next 4 tr, fasten off.

Miss centre 10 tr on front, join black in next tr, (1 dc 2 ch) in same tr as join, 1 tr in each of last 4 tr, fasten off.

Miss next 3 tr from front, join black to next tr, (1 dc 2 ch) in same tr as join, 1 tr in each of last 9 tr. Work 3 rows more in tr.

Next row: (1 dc 2 ch) in 1st tr, 1 tr in each of last 4 tr, fasten off. Sew shoulder seams.

SLEEVES

With 3.50 mm (No. 9) hook, RS facing, join a contrast colour to centre tr of 3 tr at underarm, 1 ch, evenly work 24 dc around armhole, sl st to 1st dc, TURN, 3 ch, 1 tr in each dc to end, sl st to top of 3 ch, TURN. Cont in rnds of tr in this way for further 8 rnds, fasten off.

Work same way for other Sleeve.

TRIM AND BUTTON LOOPS

With 3.50 mm (No. 9) hook and RS facing, join black to lower end of back opening. Smoothly work in dc to neck corner, 2 dc in corner, work in dc around neck edge to next corner, 1 dc in corner, 3 ch, miss 1st tr row, work in dc over next 2 rows of tr, 3 ch, miss 1 tr row, work in dc to end, TURN, 1 ch, work 1 dc in each dc to end AT SAME TIME work 3 dc in each ch loop and 2 dc at each neck corner. Fasten off. Sew on buttons.

APRON

Leaving one long side free for waistband, sew lace on three other sides. Gather top edge and attach to centre of 46 cm (18 in) long ribbon.

BONNET

Place 17 cm (6³/₄ in) squares tog, one on top of the other. Mark 3 cm (1¹/₄ in) down each side from 3 corners. Cut off marked triangle at 3 corners for head section, keeping 1 corner intact for ear sections. Sew 2 pieces together from 1 cut-off corner through 2nd one and around past 3rd one. Open out and turn to right side. Attach lace around open lower edge. Gather across corners above ear sections, 5 cm (2 in) inside each corner. Gather centre head seam for 7.5 cm (3 in) from lower edge for centre back.

HAIR AND RINGLETS

Wind dark brown yarn 100 times around cardboard and lightly press on both sides of cardboard. Tie ends like a skein. Slip yarn off cardboard into a plastic bag. Sew across width at centre. Cut 6 lengths of wool, each 40.5 cm (16 in) long. Hold ends firmly in each hand and twist wool until it coils up on itself. Arrange coils as Ringlets, tucking in under Hair at a tied end. Make second set of Ringlets for other tied end. Securely attach Hair to Head. With wool sewing needle, stitch eyes and mouth.

YUKIO THE JAPANESE DOLL

FIRST FOOT AND LEG

With 3.25 mm (No. 10) needles and natural, cast on 44 sts. Work in st st for 4 rows.
Shape foot
1st row: K20, K2 tog tbl, TURN.
***2nd row:** Sl1, P9, P2 tog, TURN.
3rd row: Sl1, K9, K2 tog tbl, TURN.
Rep last 2 rows 5 times, then 2nd row once more. 30 sts.
Next row: Sl1, knit to end of work.
Next row: P30.

MATERIALS

Yarn: For doll: 8 ply pure wool 50 g (2 oz) balls: 1¹/₂ balls in natural
For kimono and sandals: 5 ply pure wool crepe 50 g (2 oz) balls: 1 ball green
Notions: Set of four 3.25 (3¹/₄) mm (No. 10) knitting needles; one pair of 3.75 (3³/₄) mm (No. 9) knitting needles; 5 ply pure wool crepe 50 g (2 oz) balls: 1 ball black for hair and sandals; polyester fibre for filling; 5 cm x 50 cm (2 in x 20 in) ribbon for obi sash; 21 cm x 8 cm (8¹/₄ in x 3 in) cardboard; small quantity of red yarn for mouth; thin plastic bag; freezer marker pen; 2 buttons to fasten arms

MEASUREMENT

41 cm (16 in) high

SPECIAL ABBREVIATION

M1= Make 1 stitch: insert right hand needle point from back of work under horizontal loop before next st, lift it up then insert left hand needle point into front of it and knit from this position

NOTE

Feet, legs, body and head are worked in one piece

Work 38 rows more. Cast off 6 sts at beg of next 2 rows. 18 sts*. Break off yarn. Leave sts on needle.

SECOND FOOT AND LEG

Work as for First Foot and Leg until 4 rows of st st have been worked.
Shape foot
1st row: K33, K2 tog tbl, TURN.
Work as for first Foot and Leg from * to *.
Do not break off yarn. Leave work aside.
CROTCH
With 3.25 mm (No. 10) needles and natural, cast on 6 sts. Work 12 rows st st. Break off yarn. With RS facing, slip these 6 sts onto end of Second Leg. Ret to beg of Second Leg and cont for body as follows:
1st rnd: With 1st needle K13, with 2nd needle K5, K6 over Crotch, K5 from other leg, with 3rd needle K13, pick up 6 sts along RS row of cast-on edge of Crotch. 48 sts. Slip last 3 sts onto 4th needle. First of these 3 sts is beg of rnds and is centre back. First 3 sts for next rnd are already worked. Cont in rnds of st st by knitting every rnd. Work 2 rnds.
Next rnd: K2, (M1, K4) rep to last 2 sts, M1, K2. 60 sts.
Work 6 rnds straight.
Shape back opening
Next row: (Knit and inc 1 st) in first st, knit to last st, (knit and inc 1 st) in last st, 62 sts, TURN.
Working in rows, cont in st st for further 25 rows, ending with WS row. Dec 1 st each end of next row. 60 sts. Cont in rnds of st st as before. Work 4 rnds.
Shape neck
Evenly dec 10 sts on next and every foll 3rd rnd until 30 sts rem. Work 2 rnds straight.
Next rnd: (K1 tbl) rep to end.
Cont for head as follows:
Cont in rnds of st st, evenly inc 15 sts on every 3rd rnd twice, 60 sts. Evenly inc 12 sts on foll 3rd rnd. 72 sts.
Work 12 rnds straight.
Shape cheeks
Next rnd: K21, (K2 tog) 6 times, K6, (sl1, K1, psso) 6 times, K21. 60 sts.
Keeping beg of rnd at beg of 1st needle as before, rearrange sts evenly on 3 needles. Cont in rnds of st st. Work 12 rnds straight. Evenly dec 10 sts on next and every foll 2nd rnd until 10 sts rem. Work 1 rnd on rem 10 sts. Break off, leaving length of yarn. Thread end of yarn through rem sts, draw up tightly and securely fasten off.

HANDS AND ARMS

With 3.25 mm (No. 10) needles and natural, cast on 2 sts. Work in st st, inc 1 st at each end of 1st and 3rd rows. 6 sts. Work 3 rows straight *. Break off yarn. Leave aside. Make another piece the same to * and cont as follows:

Next row: Cast on 3 sts, knit all sts, then K6 over other piece.

Next row: Cast on 3 sts, purl all sts. 18 sts.

Next row: Sl1, K1, psso, K6, M1, K2, M1, K6, K2 tog.

Next row: Purl.

Rep last 2 rows twice. Work 2 rows straight, then inc 1 st at each end of next row. 20 sts. Work 11 rows straight.

Next row: K1, M1, K7, K2 tog, sl1, K1, psso, K7, M1, K1.

Work 3 rows straight, then rep last 4 rows twice.

Shape top

1st row: (Sl1, K1, psso, K6, K2 tog) twice.

2nd, 4th, 6th rows: Purl.

3rd row: (Sl1, K1, psso, K4, K2 tog) twice.

5th row: (Sl1, K1, psso, K2, K2 tog) twice.

Cast/bind off. Make another one the same.

SOLES

Make 2

With 3.25 mm (No. 10) needles and natural, cast on 5 sts. Work in st st, inc 1 st each end of 1st and 3rd rows, 9 sts, then on every foll 8th row twice. 13 sts. Work 3 rows straight, then dec 1 st each end of next and foll 2nd row once more.

Next row: (Toe end) P2 tog, then cast/bind off to last 2 sts, P2 tog and cast/bind off.

KIMONO

With 3.75 mm (No. 9) needles and green, cast on 100 sts.

1st row: (K1, P1) rep to end.

2nd row: (P1, K1) rep to end.

Rep last 2 rows 3 times for Moss st.

Next row: Moss 7 sts, knit to last 7 sts, Moss 7 sts.

Next row: Moss 7 sts, purl to last 7 sts, Moss 7 sts.

Rep last 2 rows until work is 7.5 cm (3 in) from beg, ending with WS row.

Shape front

1st row: Cast on 5 sts, (K1, P1) twice, K1 over cast-on sts, Moss 7 sts, knit to last 7 sts, Moss 7 sts.

2nd row: Cast on 5 sts, (P1, K1) twice and P1 over cast-on sts, Moss 7 sts, purl to last 12 sts, Moss 7 sts, P1, (K1, P1) twice. 110 sts.

3rd row: (K1, P1) twice, sl1, K1, psso, Moss 6 sts, knit to last 12 sts, Moss 6 sts, K2 tog, (P1, K1) twice.

4th row: P1, (K1, P1) twice, Moss 6 sts, purl to last 11 sts, Moss 6 sts, P1, (K1, P1) twice.

5th row: (K1, P1) twice, sl1, K1, psso, Moss 5 sts, knit to last 11 sts, Moss 5 sts, K2 tog, (P1, K1) twice.

Working in rib at each end as set, cont to dec 1 st in this way, working 1 st less in Moss st patt on every foll 2nd row until all Moss sts have been dec, then cont to dec in same way 4 sts inside each end and working 2 sts less in st st on every foll 2nd row until 88 sts rem. Work 1 row.

Divide for right front

Next row: (K1, P1) twice, sl1, K1, psso, K17, TURN, leave rem sts on holder.

Next row: Cast on 16 sts for Sleeve, (P1, K1) twice, P12 over cast-on sts, purl to last 4 sts, (K1, P1) twice. 38 sts.

Next row: (K1, P1) twice, sl1, K1, psso, knit to last 4 sts, (P1, K1) twice.

Next row: (P1, K1) twice, purl to last 4 sts, (K1, P1) twice.

Rep last 2 rows 5 times. 32 sts.

Work 10 rows straight. Leave sts on holder, or cast/bind off.

Ret to rem sts, join yarn to next st and cont for Back as follows:

1st row: Cast on 16 sts, (K1, P1) twice, K12 over cast-on sts, K42, TURN.

2nd row: Cast on 16 sts, (P1, K1) twice, P12 over cast-on sts, purl to last 4 sts, (K1, P1) twice. 74 sts.

3rd row: (K1, P1) twice, knit to last 4 sts, (P1, K1) twice.

4th row: (P1, K1) twice, purl to last 4 sts, (K1, P1) twice.

Rep last 2 rows 8 times.

Shape neck

1st row: (K1, P1) twice, K26, cast/bind off centre 14 sts, knit to last 4 sts (P1, K1) twice.

Cont on last 30 sts and dec 1 st at neck edge on next 3 rows. Leave rem 27 sts on holder or cast/bind off.

Ret to rem 30 sts on back, rejoin yarn at neck edge and complete to match other side.

Ret to rem 23 sts for left front, rejoin yarn and cont as follows:

1st row: Cast on 16 sts, (K1, P1) twice, knit to last 6 sts, K2 tog, (P1, K1) twice.

2nd row: (P1, K1) twice, purl to last 4 sts, (K1, P1) twice. 38 sts.

3rd row: (K1, P1) twice, knit to last 6 sts, K2 tog, (P1, K1) twice.

Rep last 2 rows 5 times. 32 sts rem.

Work 10 rows straight. Leave sts on holder or cast/bind off.

Leaving 5 sts of rib at neck edge for neckband, graft shoulder sts tog or sew shoulder seams. With 3.75 mm (No. 9) needles, rejoin yarn at inner edge of 5 sts and inc 1 st in first st. 6 sts.

Work in rib as before until band fits to centre back neck. Cast/bind off in rib. Work other side the same. Neatly join bands tog, then attach around neck edge.

SANDALS

Make 4

With 3.25 mm (No. 10) needles and black, cast on 10 sts. Work in st st, inc 1 st each end of 1st 4 rows. 18 sts.

Work 26 rows straight, then dec 1 st each end of next 4 rows. Cast/bind off.

Using 3 strands each of green and black, make 2 twist cords 22 cm (8$\frac{1}{2}$ in) long, then pull each end of cord through 4th st from each side edge at 8th row from beg of Sandal. Secure ends on purl side of piece. With right sides tog and keeping cord inside, backstitch two sole pieces together, leaving small opening for turning. Turn right side out and close opening.

TO MAKE UP

Main section: Sew side seam of each Leg, then join cast-off edge of Legs to each side of Crotch. Sew Soles in place. Fill firmly, rearranging filling with needle point for better shaping. Close back opening. Leaving 3 cm (1$\frac{1}{4}$ in) open at top, sew outer edges of Hand and Arm. Fill. Insert button in top edge of each arm to secure stitches. With thick cotton securely attach

---

HINT

When you have finished with your knitting for the day take care to finish at the end of a row. If you put your work aside for a number of hours, having stopped in the middle of a row, you may find the knitting fabric is uneven or there may be a gap. If you get into the habit of always working to the end of a row you will never have this problem.

arms through body and through buttons. Close openings. Embroider eyes with black and mouth with red. Tie ribbon around waist for Obi sash. Place Sandals on feet, taking cords over feet and catching at centre front between 'toes'. Catch cords to feet at several points to keep Sandals in place.

To make hair: Evenly wind black yarn lengthways around cardboard until it is covered and cont until desired thickness is reached. Slip yarn carefully off cardboard into plastic bag. Mark centre of hair and stitch along this line with black thread. Stitch again. Remove plastic bag and cut through loops at each end. Place centre line of hair as centre parting on head and attach in place. Arrange and trim hair as desired.

EDWARD THE GUARDSMAN

MATERIALS
Yarn: 5 ply pure new wool 50 g (2 oz) balls: 1½ balls black; 1½ balls natural; 1 ball red; small quantity yellow
Notions: One 3.00 (3) mm (No. 11) crochet hook; polyester fibre for filling; 2 flat buttons for eyes; 5 gold buttons for Jacket; hat elastic for Trousers; small pompom 1.25 cm (½ in) in diameter; craft glue; small buckle 1.5 cm (½ in) wide

MEASUREMENT
40.5 cm (16 in) high

HEAD AND BODY
With 3.00 mm (No. 11) hook and black, make 5 ch, sl st to 1st ch to form circle.
1st rnd: Work 1 ch, 2 dc in each ch to end, sl st to 1st dc.
2nd rnd: Work 1 ch, 2 dc in each of 10 dc, sl st to 1st dc.
Work in rnds of dc, evenly inc 10 dc on every foll 2nd rnd until there are 50 dc. Cont 11 rnds more in dc in spiral without working sl st to join rnds. Work sl st to next dc at end of 11th rnd.
Next rnd: 1 ch, 1 dc in front loop of each dc to end, sl st to 1st dc.

Working into both loops of each dc, work 3 rnds more in dc, fasten off. Turn down last 3 rnds of dc to outside, join natural to back loop of 1st dc of 11th rnd and cont to work for face as follows:
Next rnd: 1 ch 1 dc in same place as join, 1 dc in back loop of each dc to end, sl st to 1st dc, place marker in last dc to denote end of rnd.
Cont in rnds of dc in spiral without working sl st to join rnds and work 8 rnds more. Evenly dec 10 dc on next and every foll 2nd rnd until 20 dc rem. Cont 5 rnds more on these rem 20 dc in spiral, evenly inc 10 dc on next rnd and foll 2nd rnd once more, then on foll 2nd rnd evenly inc 5 dc. 45 dc. Cont to work 26 rnds more in dc in spiral, sl st to next dc, fasten off.

LEGS
Make 2
With 3.00 mm (No. 11) hook and black, make 5 ch, sl st to 1st ch to form circle. On next rnd, work 1 ch, 2 dc in each of 5 ch, sl st to 1st dc.
Cont in rnds of dc, evenly inc 5 dc on next 2 rnds. 20 dc.
Work 5 rnds in dc on these 20 dc, break off. Join in natural, and cont to work 36 rnds more in dc in spiral. Fasten off.

ARMS
Make 2
With 3.00 mm (No. 11) hook and natural, make 5 ch, sl st to 1st ch to form circle, 1 ch, 2 dc in each of 5 ch, sl st to 1st dc.
Cont in rnds of dc and evenly inc 5 dc on next rnd. 15 dc.
Cont on these 15 dc for 20 rnds in spiral.
Next rnd: 1 dc in each of 1st 3 dc, 1 h tr in each of next 2 dc, 1 tr in each of next 6 dc, 1 h tr in each of next 2 dc, 1 dc in each of last 2 dc.
Next rnd: 1 dc in each of 15 sts.
Rep last 2 rnds 3 times more, sl st to next dc, fasten off.

TO MAKE UP
Fill Body, Head, Legs and Arms. Matching dc to dc, join every dc of one Leg to lower end of Body. Catch 2 dc at centre of Body for crotch, then join other Leg in same way. Securely attach Arms to Body.
With hook and black yarn, make 34 ch, 1 dc in 2nd ch from hook, 1 dc in each ch to end, fasten off. Sew this cord from side to side of head, passing under chin. Sew 2 flat buttons for eyes under brim of helmet, covering half of eyes. Glue on small pompom for nose.

JACKET
Worked in tr. With red, make 54 ch.
1st row: 1 tr in 4th ch from hook, 1 tr in each ch to end. 52 tr, counting 3 ch as 1 tr.
2nd row: 3 ch, 1 tr in 2nd and in each foll tr, ending with 1 tr in top of 3 ch.
Rep last row 7 times more.
Divide for Fronts and Back
1st row: 3 ch, 1 tr in 2nd and in each foll tr until there are 11 tr from beg, TURN.
Work 3 rows more on these 11 tr.
Next row: Sl st in each of 1st 6 tr, 3 ch, 1 tr in each of last 5 tr, fasten off.
Miss 4 tr from front, rejoin red to next tr and cont for back as follows:
1st row: 3 ch, 1 tr in each of next 21 tr, TURN.
Work 3 rows more on these 22 tr.
Next row: 3 ch for 1st tr, 1 tr in each of next 5 tr, fasten off.
Miss centre 10 tr for back neck, rejoin red to next tr, 3 ch, 1 tr in each of last 5 tr, fasten off.
Miss next 4 tr from back, rejoin red to next tr, 3 ch, 1 tr in each of last 10 tr, then work 3 rows more on these 11 tr. On next row, work 3 ch for 1st tr, 1 tr in each of next 5 tr, fasten off.
Sew shoulder seams.
SLEEVES
With RS facing, join red to a tr at underarm, 1 ch, 1 dc in same tr as join, evenly

work 24 dc in all around armhole, sl st to 1st dc, TURN.

Next rnd: 3 ch, 1 tr in each dc to end, sl st to top of 3 ch, TURN.

Work 8 rnds more in tr, sl st to top of 3 ch, fasten off.

Work same for other Sleeve.

TRIM

With RS facing, join red to foundation ch at centre back, 1 ch, 1 dc in same ch as join, 1 dc in each ch to corner, (1 dc, 2 ch, 1 dc) in corner, smoothly work in dc along front edge, (1 dc, 2 ch, 1 dc) in corner, smoothly work in dc round neck edge, (1 dc, 2 ch, 1 dc) in corner, *3 ch, miss 1 tr row, work in dc over next 2 rows of tr, rep from * 3 times more, 3 ch, miss last row of tr, (1 dc, 2 ch, 1 dc) in lower corner, 1 dc in each foundation ch to end, sl st to 1st dc, TURN.

Next rnd: 1 ch, 1 dc in same dc as sl st, 1 dc in each dc to end AT SAME TIME work (1 dc, 2 ch, 1 dc) in 2 ch sp at each of 4 corners and 3 dc in each of 3 ch loops, sl st to 1st dc, fasten off.

Sew on 5 buttons. With hook and yellow yarn, make 2 epaulets by working 5 ch, 1 dc in 2nd ch from hook, 1 dc in each of next 2 ch, 3 dc in last ch, working on other side of ch work 1 dc in each of next 2 ch, 2 dc in same place as 1st dc, sl st to 1st dc, fasten off. Attach epaulets in place.

TROUSERS

Worked in tr. With black, make 28 ch, sl st to 1st ch to form circle.

1st rnd: (RS) 3 ch, 1 tr in each ch to end, sl st to top of 3 ch. 28 tr, counting 3 ch as 1 tr, TURN.

2nd rnd: 3 ch, 1 tr in each tr to end, sl st to top of 3 ch, TURN.

Rep last rnd 13 times more, ending on RS.

Next rnd: 3 ch, 2 tr in next tr, 1 tr in each tr to last 2 tr, 2 tr in next tr, 1 tr in last tr, sl st to top of 3 ch. 30 tr, counting 3 ch as 1 tr. Fasten off. Place marker in 3rd tr before and after 3 ch and these 7 trs form crotch later on.

Make another one the same and place markers as 1st one. Join 2 Legs together over these 7 marked trs.

Cont for upper section as follows:

With RS facing, rejoin black to left marker of a Leg, 3 ch and 1 tr in same place as join, 2 tr in next tr, 1 tr in each of next 21 tr, 2 tr in next tr, 2 tr in next marker of same Leg, 2 tr in next marker of other Leg, 2 tr in next tr, 1 tr in each of next 21 tr, 2 tr in next tr, 2 tr in last marker of same Leg, sl st to top

of 3 ch. 58 tr, counting 3 ch as 1 tr, TURN.

Next rnd: 3 ch, 1 tr in each tr to end, sl st to top of 3 ch, TURN.

Next rnd: 3 ch, 1 tr in each tr to end AT SAME TIME (inc 1 tr) twice at centre back and front of Trousers, sl st to top of 3 ch. 62 tr. TURN.

Cont to work 4 rnds more, fasten off.

With yellow yarn, and wool sewing needle, stitch a row of chain stitch along outside of Legs. Cut elastic and thread through spaces between trs round top edge and join ends together.

BELT

With yellow yarn, make 5 ch, 1 tr in 4th ch from hook, 1 tr in last ch. 3 tr.

Work 34 rows more in tr, or length required for Belt, fasten off. Attach buckle to one end. With yellow yarn, make 13 ch, 1 dc in 2nd ch from hook, 1 dc in each ch to end, fasten off. Join ends of this cord and attach to Belt as a belt-carrier.

ROSALITA, THE SPANISH DOLL

MATERIALS

Yarn: 5 ply pure wool crepe 50 g (2 oz) balls: 1½ balls natural; 1 ball red; 1 ball black; small quantity yellow

Notions: One each 3.50 (3½) mm (No. 9) and 3.00 (3) mm (No. 11) crochet hooks; polyester fibre for filling; 6 black buttons for dress; 2 small black buttons for eyes; 2 gold metal buttons for earrings; 16.5 cm x 5 cm (6½ x 2 in) cardboard; thin plastic bag

MEASUREMENT

38 cm (15 in) high

SPECIAL ABBREVIATIONS

(1 dc 2 ch) at beg of tr row stands for 1 tr, and always work the last tr on next row in top of (1 dc 2 ch)

dec 1 tr = (yoh, insert hook in next st, yoh and draw a loop through, yoh and draw through 2 loops on hook) twice, yoh and draw through 3 loops on hook

HEAD AND BODY

With 3.00 mm (No. 11) hook and natural, make 5 ch, sl st to 1st ch to form circle.

1st rnd: 1 ch, 2 dc in each of 5 ch, sl st to 1st dc.

2nd rnd: 1 ch, 2 dc in each of 10 dc, sl st to 1st dc.

3rd rnd: 1 ch, 1 dc in each dc to end.

4th rnd: 1 ch, *1 dc in next dc, 2 dc in next dc, rep from * to end, sl st to 1st dc.

5th rnd: 1 ch, work in dc and evenly inc 10 dc, sl st to 1st dc. 40 dc.

6th rnd: Work as 3rd rnd.

7th and 8th rnds: Rep 5th and 6th rnds once. 50 dc.

Work 14 rnds in dc in spiral without working sl st, then evenly dec 10 dc on next and every foll 2nd rnd until 20 dc rem. Work 5 rnds on these 20 dc, then evenly inc 10 dc on next and foll 2nd rnd once more. On foll 2nd rnd evenly inc 5 dc. 45 dc.

Cont to work 26 rnds in dc in spiral without working sl st, fasten off.

LEGS

Make 2

With 3.00 mm (No. 11) hook and black, make 5 ch, sl st to 1st ch to form circle, 1 ch, 2 dc in each of 5 ch, sl st to 1st dc. 10 dc. Cont in rnds of dc, evenly inc 5 dc on next 2 rnds. 20 dc.

Cont for 5 rnds without further inc. Break off.

Join natural, cont to work 36 rnds more in spiral without working sl st, fasten off.

ARMS

Make 2

With 3.00 mm (No. 11) hook and natural, make 5 ch, sl st to 1st ch to form circle. On next rnd, work 1 ch, 2 dc in each of 5 ch, sl st to 1st dc. 10 dc.

Cont in rnds of dc, evenly inc 5 dc on next rnd. 15 dc. Cont without further inc for 22 rnds in spiral.

Next rnd: 1 dc in each of next 2 dc, 1 h tr in each of next 2 dc, 1 tr in each of next 6 dc, 1 h tr in each of next 2 dc, 1 dc in each of last 3 dc.

Next rnd: 1 ch, 1 dc in each of 15 sts.

Rep last 2 rnds 3 times, fasten off.

Fill Body, Head, Legs and Arms. Matching dc to dc, join every dc of Leg to lower end of Body. Catch 2 dc tog at centre of Body for crotch. Cont to join other Leg as before. Securely attach Arms in place.

DRESS

Worked in tr. With 3.50 mm (No. 9) hook and red, make 66 ch.

1st row: 1 tr in 4th ch from hook, 1 tr in each ch to end. 64 tr.
2nd row: (1 dc 2 ch) in 1st tr, 1 tr in each tr, ending with last tr to top of 3 ch.
3rd row: (1 dc 2 ch) in 1st tr, 1 tr in each tr, ending with last tr to top of (1 dc 2 ch).
4th, 5th rows: Rep 3rd row twice.
6th row: (1 dc 2 ch) in 1st tr, 1 tr in each of next 5 tr, *dec 1 tr, 1 tr in each of next 8 tr, rep from * 5 times more, ending with 1 tr in each of last 6 tr instead of 8 tr.
7th to 9th rows: Rep 3rd row 3 times.
10th row: (1 dc 2 ch) in 1st tr, 1 tr in each of next 2 tr, *dec 1 tr, 1 tr in each of next 8 tr, rep from * 5 times more, ending with 1 tr in each of last 3 tr instead of 8 tr.
11th to 13th rows: Rep 3rd row 3 times.
14th row: (1 dc 2 ch) in 1st tr, 1 tr in each of next 4 tr, *dec 1 tr, 1 tr in each of next 6 tr, rep from * 5 times more, ending with 1 tr in each of last 5 tr instead of 6 tr. 46 tr.
Work 3 rows straight
Divide for backs and front
1st row: (1 dc 2 ch) in 1st tr, 1 tr in each of next 9 tr, TURN.
Work 3 rows more on these 10 tr.
Next row: Sl st in each of 1st 6 tr, 3 ch, 1 tr in each of last 4 tr, fasten off.
Miss next 3 tr from back, join red to next tr,

and cont for front as follows:
1st row: (1 dc 2 ch) in same tr as join, 1 tr in each of next 19 tr, TURN.
Work 3 rows straight on these 20 tr.
Next row: (1 dc 2 ch) in 1st tr, 1 tr in each of next 4 tr, fasten off.
Miss next 10 tr on front, join red in next tr, (1 dc 2 ch) in same tr as join, 1 tr in each of last 4 tr, fasten off.
Miss next 3 tr from front, join red in next tr, (1 dc 2 ch) in same tr as join, 1 tr in each of last 9 tr. Work 3 rows straight on these 10 tr.
Next row: (1 dc 2 ch) in 1st tr, 1 tr in each of next 4 tr, fasten off.
SLEEVES
Join shoulder seams. With RS facing, 3.50 mm (No. 9) hook, join red to centre tr at underarm, 1 ch, evenly work 30 dc around armhole, sl st to 1st dc.
Next rnd: 3 ch, 1 tr in each dc to end, sl st to top of 3 ch, TURN.
Next rnd: 3 ch, 1 tr in each tr to end, sl st to top of 3 ch, TURN.
Rep last rnd once.
Next rnd: With RS facing, 5 ch, 1 tr in next tr, (2 ch, 1 tr in next tr) rep to end, 2 ch, sl st to 3rd of 5 ch, break off.
Next rnd: With RS facing, join black to 1st tr, (3 ch, 1 dc in next sp) rep to end, 3 ch, sl st to 1st ch of 1st loop, fasten off.
Work other Sleeve the same.
FRILL FOR LOWER EDGE
With 3.50 mm (No. 9) hook, RS facing join red to 1st foundation ch, 5 ch, 1 tr in next ch, (2 ch, 1 tr in next ch) rep to end, break off.
Next row: With WS facing, join black to 1st sp, (3 ch, 1 dc in next sp) rep to end, fasten off.
For second row of Frill work in 3rd row of tr above foundation ch. With RS facing, 3.50 mm (No. 9) hook, join red in stem of 1st tr, 5 ch, * lift stem of next tr and work 1 tr round it, 2 ch, rep from * ending with last tr around stem of last tr, break off.
With black, work last row as on Frill for Lower Edge.
TRIM AND BUTTON LOOPS
With 3.50 mm (No. 9) hook and RS facing, join red to foundation ch of back opening. Smoothly work in dc along back opening to neck corner, 2 dc in corner, smoothly work in dc around neck edge to next corner, 1 dc in corner, (3 ch, miss 1 tr row, work in dc over next 2 tr rows) 6 times in all, work in dc to foundation ch row, TURN.
Next row: 1 ch, 1 dc in each dc to end, AT

SAME TIME work 3 dc in each ch loop and 2 dc at each neck corner, fasten off.
Sew on buttons.

SNOOD
Work in dc. With 3.50 mm (No. 9) hook and black, make 5 ch, sl st to 1st ch, 1 ch, 2 dc in each of 5 ch, sl st to 1st dc. On next rnd, work 1 ch, 2 dc in each of 10 dc, sl st to 1st dc. Work 1 rnd without inc.
Next rnd: 1 ch, (2 dc in next dc, 1 dc in next dc) 10 times. 30 dc.
Work 4 rnds straight, fasten off.
With yellow and wool sewing needle, stitch a few flowers, using lazy daisy stitch on Snood.

HAIR
Wind black yarn around cardboard lengthways until width is covered, then cont winding until desired thickness is obtained, break off. Press while it is still on cardboard. Carefully slip off cardboard and cut one looped end. Keeping strands of yarn together, slip them into plastic bag. Sew along foldline, then remove plastic bag. Fold length in half at sewing line, and place it on top of Head with foldline parallel to forehead. Securely attach to Head in this position. Make another Hair piece and place it over the 1st one with foldline at a right angle to 1st one. Smooth strands over Head to back and securely tie all strands at back of neck in a bun. Slip all ends into Snood and secure to back of neck.

TO MAKE UP
Sew on buttons for eyes, and with wool sewing needle and red, stitch mouth. Sew on metal buttons for earrings.

HINT

Distributing the stuffing evenly throughout the toy can sometimes be quite difficult, especially if you need to get into narrow spaces, such as arms and legs. You can use the point of one of your needles or, even better, the blunt end of a pencil. Wrapping the end with sticky tape, sticky side out, makes the job even easier.

HANSEL AND GRETEL

MATERIALS

For Hansel: 8 ply pure wool 50 g (2 oz) balls: 1½ balls natural; ¼ ball black; ½ ball light brown for Hair; set of four 3.25 (3¼) mm (No. 10) knitting needles

For Hansel's clothes: 5 ply pure wool 50 g (2 oz) balls: 1½ balls brown for shorts; ½ ball green for shirt

Notions: One pair of 3.75 (3¾) mm (No. 9) knitting needles; polyester fibre for filling; 21 cm x 8 cm (8 in x 3 in) cardboard; 2 buttons for eyes; 2 buttons for fastening arms; 2 buttons for Shorts; 4 buttons for Shirt; small quantity of red yarn for mouth; thin plastic bag; chalk

For Gretel: Same as for Hansel but use set of four 3.00 (3) mm (No. 11) knitting needles instead of 3.25 (3¼) mm (No. 10) needles; ½ ball 8 ply yarn in gold for Hair

For Gretel's clothes: 5 ply pure new wool 50 g (2 oz) balls: ½ ball red; ½ ball blue; small quantity white

Notions: One pair of 3.75 (3¾) mm (No. 9) knitting needles; 3 press studs; polyester fibre for filling; 2 buttons for eyes; 2 buttons for fastening arms; 21 cm x 8 cm (8 in x 3 in) cardboard; thin plastic bag; chalk

MEASUREMENTS

Hansel: 41 cm (16 in) high
Gretel: 38 cm (15 in) high

SPECIAL ABBREVIATION

M1 = Make one stitch: insert right hand needle point from back of work and under horizontal loop before next st, lift it up then insert left hand needle point in front loop and knit from this position

NOTE

Feet, legs, body and head are worked in one piece

FIRST FOOT AND LEG

For both dolls

Using 3.00 mm (No. 11) needles for Gretel and 3.25 mm (No. 10) needles for Hansel. With 2 needles and black, cast on 44 sts. Work in st st for 4 rows.

Shape foot

1st row: K20, K2 tog tbl, TURN.

* **2nd row:** Sl1, P9, P2 tog, TURN.

3rd row: Sl1, K9, K2 tog tbl, TURN.

Rep last 2 rows 5 times, then 2nd row once more. 30 sts.

Next row: Sl1, knit to end of work.
Change to natural and beg with purl row, cont in st st for 39 rows. Cast/bind off 6 sts at beg of next 2 rows. 18 sts *. Break off yarn. Leave sts on needle.

SECOND FOOT AND LEG

Work as for First Foot and Leg until 4 rows of st st from beg have been worked.

Shape foot

1st row: K33, K2 tog tbl, TURN.
Work as for First Foot from * to *. Do not break off yarn and leave work aside.

CROTCH AND BODY

With 2 needles and natural, cast on 6 sts. Work 12 rows in st st. Break off yarn. With RS facing, slip these 6 sts onto end of Second Leg. Ret to beg of Second Leg and cont for Body as follows:

1st rnd: With 1st needle K13, with 2nd needle K5, K6 over Crotch, K5 from other Leg, with 3rd needle K13, pick up 6 sts along RS row of cast-on edge of Crotch. 48 sts.

Slip last 3 sts onto 4th needle. First of these 3 sts is beg of rnds and is centre back. First 3 sts for next rnd are already worked.

Cont in rnds of st st by knitting every rnd. Work 2 rnds.

Next rnd: K2, (M1, K4) rep to last 2 sts, M1, K2. 60 sts.

Work 6 rnds straight.

Shape back opening

Next row: (Knit and inc 1 st) in first st, knit to last st, (knit and inc 1 st) in last st. 62 sts. TURN.

Working in rows, cont in st st for further 25 rows ending with WS row. Dec 1 st at each end of next row. 60 sts. Cont in rnds of st st as before and work 4 rnds.

Shape neck

Evenly dec 10 sts on next and every foll 3rd rnd until 30 sts rem, then work 2 rnds straight.

Next rnd: (K1 tbl) rep to end.
Cont for Head as follows:

Cont in rnds of st st, evenly inc 15 sts on every 3rd rnd twice. 60 sts. Evenly inc 12 sts on foll 3rd rnd. 72 sts.
Work 12 rnds straight.

Shape cheeks

Next rnd: K21, (K2 tog) 6 times, K6, (sl1, K1, psso) 6 times, K21. 60 sts.
Keeping beg of rnd at beg of 1st needle as before, rearrange sts evenly on 3 needles. Cont in rnds of st st. Work 12 rnds straight, evenly dec 10 sts on next and every foll 2nd rnd until 10 sts rem. Work 1 rnd on rem 10 sts. Break off, leaving a length of yarn. Thread end of yarn through rem sts and draw up tightly. Fasten off securely.

HANDS AND ARMS

For both dolls

With 2 needles and natural, cast on 2 sts. Work in st st. Inc 1 st each end of 1st and 3rd rows. 6 sts. Then work 3 rows straight*. Break off yarn and leave work aside. Make another piece the same as far as * and cont as follows:

Next row: Cast on 3 sts, knit all sts, then K6 over other piece.

Next row: Cast on 3 sts, purl all sts. 18 sts.

Next row: Sl1, K1, psso, K6, M1, K2, M1, K6, K2 tog.

Next row: Purl.

Rep last 2 rows twice. Work 2 rows straight, then inc 1 st at each end of next row. 20 sts. Work 11 rows straight.

Next row: K1, M1, K7, K2 tog, sl1, K1, psso, K7, M1, K1.

Work 3 rows straight. Rep last 4 rows twice.

Shape top

1st row: (Sl1, K1, psso, K6, K2 tog) twice.

2nd, 4th, 6th rows: Purl.

3rd row: (Sl1, K1, psso, K4, K2 tog) twice.

5th row: (Sl1, K1, psso, K2, K2 tog) twice.
Cast/bind off. Make another one the same.

SOLES

Make 2 for each doll

With 2 needles and black, cast on 5 sts. Work in st st. Inc 1 st each end of 1st and 3rd rows. 9 sts. Cont inc on every foll 8th row twice. 13 sts.

Work 3 rows straight, then dec 1 st each end of next and foll 2nd row once more.

Next row: (Toe end) P2 tog, then cast/bind off to last 2 sts, P2 tog. Cast/bind off.

HANSEL'S SHIRT

With pair of 3.75 mm (No. 9) needles and green, cast on 76 sts. Work 4 rows in K1, P1 rib. Change to st st and work until rib is

6 cm (2¹/₂ in) from beg ending with WS row.

Divide for right front

Next row: K13, TURN.

Cont on these 13 sts until work is 9.5 cm (3³/₄ in) from beg ending at armhole edge.

Next row: P7, TURN, leave rem 6 sts on a piece of wool for Neckband. Cont on these 7 sts for further 4 rows. Cast/bind off. Ret to rem 63 sts, and leave next 10 sts on a piece of wool for Sleeve. Rejoin green to next st and work for back as follows:

Next row: K30, TURN.

Cont on these 30 sts until 9.5 cm (3³/₄ in) from beg ending with WS row.

Next row: K7, TURN.

Work 3 rows on these 7 sts and cast/bind off. Slip next 16 sts of back onto a piece of wool for Neckband. Rejoin green to next st and work 4 rows, then cast/bind off.

Ret to rem 23 sts. Leave next 10 sts on a piece of wool for Sleeve. Rejoin green to next st and work left front to match right front, reversing shapings.

SLEEVES

With RS facing, a pair of 3.75 mm (No. 9) needles and green, beg and end at shoulder edge, evenly pick up 16 sts down armhole edge, K10 from underarm, pick up 16 sts along other side of armhole edge, TURN. 42 sts.

1st and each alt row: Purl.

2nd row: K15, sl1, K1, psso, K8, K2 tog, K15.

4th row: K15, sl1, K1, psso, K6, K2 tog, K15.

6th row: K15, sl1, K1, psso, K4, K2 tog, K15.

8th row: K15, sl1, K1, psso, K2, K2 tog, K15.

9th row: P34.

Work in K1, P1 rib for 3 rows. Cast/bind off in rib.

RIGHT FRONT BAND

With RS facing, two 3.25 mm (No. 10) needles and green, evenly pick up 31 sts on right front edge. Work in K1, P1, rib for 3 rows. Cast/bind off in rib.

LEFT FRONT BAND

With RS facing, two 3.25 mm (No. 10) needles and green, evenly pick up 31 sts on left front edge.

1st row: P1, K1, *yfwd, K2 tog, (P1, K1) 4 times, rep from * once, yfwd, K2 tog, (P1, K1) 3 times, P1. 3 buttonholes are made, 4th one will be in Neckband.

Work 2 more rows in rib as before. Cast/bind off in rib.

NECKBAND

With flat seam, sew shoulder seams including Sleeve sections. With RS facing, two 3.25 mm (No. 10) needles and green, pick up 51 sts around neck edge including sts from pieces of wool.

1st row: P1, (K1, P1) rep to end.

2nd row: K1, (P1, K1) rep to last 4 sts, K2 tog, yrn, P1, K1.

Work 1 more row in rib and cast/bind off in rib. Sew 4 buttons on left front.

HANSEL'S SHORTS

With pair of 3.75 mm (No. 9) needles and brown, cast on 51 sts. Work in K1, P1 rib for 4 rows, then change to st st.

1st row: K4, *inc 1 st in next st, K5, rep from * ending with K4 instead of K5. 59 sts. Work 1 row. Cast/bind off 4 sts at beg of next 2 rows. Dec 1 st each end of next and every foll 2nd row until 45 sts rem. Cont on these 45 sts until piece meas 7 cm (2¾ in) from beg **, ending on WS row.

Work 4 rows in K1, P1 rib.

***Next row:** Cast/bind off 34 sts in rib, work in rib to end.

Cont on last 11 sts in rib for further 5 rows, ending at inner edge.

Next row: Rib 3 sts, yfwd, K2 tog, rib to end.

Work 2 more rows in rib. Cast/bind off in rib.

Work 2nd piece as 1st piece to ** ending on RS row. Work 4 rows in rib then cont to work as 1st piece from *** to end.

STRAPS

Make 2

With pair of 3.75 mm (No. 9) needles and brown, cast on 50 sts. Knit 3 rows. Cast/bind off.

GRETEL'S DRESS

With pair of 3.75 mm (No. 9) needles and white, cast on 105 sts.

1st row: Knit.

2nd row: K5, purl to last 5 sts, K5.

Rep last 2 rows once, break off yarn. Change to red.

Next row: K7, *insert right hand needle point into foundation row of next st and knit

from this position, K4, rep from * to last 3 sts, K3.

Next row: K5, purl to last 5 sts, K5.

Working K5 on every row at each end, cont in st st. Work until piece meas 9 cm (3½ in) from beg, ending with WS row. Break off yarn. Change to blue and two 3.00 mm (No. 11) needles. Cont as follows:

Next row: K6, (K2 tog, K1) 31 times, K6. 74 sts.

Next row: Knit.

Next row: K6, (yfwd, K2 tog) 31 times, yfwd, K6. 75 sts.

Knit 5 rows, ending with WS row.

Cont in g st and divide for front and backs as follows:

Work over 1st 15 sts only until piece meas 5 cm (2 in) from beg of blue section ending at outer edge. Cast/bind off 8 sts at beg of next row for neck. Knit 4 rows more on rem 7 sts. Cast/bind off.

Ret to rem 60 sts, slip next 10 sts onto a piece of wool for Sleeve. Rejoin blue to next st, K25, TURN.

Cont on these 25 sts for front until 5 cm (2 in) from beg of blue section, ending with WS row.

Next row: K7, cast/bind off centre 11 sts, knit to end.

Knit 4 rows more on last 7 sts. Cast/bind off. Rejoin blue to 7 sts on other side and knit 4 rows. Cast/bind off.

Ret to rem 25 sts, slip next 10 sts onto a piece of wool for other Sleeve, rejoin blue

to next st and complete to match other half, reversing shapings.

SLEEVES

With RS facing, 3.00 mm (No. 11) needles and red, beg and end at shoulder edges, evenly pick up 14 sts on armhole edge, K10 from piece of wool, pick up 14 sts on other side of armhole. 38 sts.

Beg with purl row cont in st st, and work 3 rows.

Next row: K17, K2 tog, sl1, K1, psso, K17.

Next row: Purl.

Next row: K16, K2 tog, sl1, K1, psso, K16.

Cont to dec 2 sts at underarm in this way on foll 2nd row once. Work 3 rows straight. Work in K1, P1 rib for 3 rows. Cast/bind off in rib.

TO MAKE UP

Main section both dolls: Sew inside Leg seams, then join cast off edges of Legs to side edges of crotch. Sew Soles in place. Fill firmly, pushing filling with point of needle for better shaping. Close opening. Fold Hand and Arm pieces in half. Leaving 3 cm (1¼ in) open around top edge, sew seams. Fill Arms. Insert button in top of each Arm to secure stitches. With thick cotton securely attach Arms through Body and through buttons. Close openings. Sew on buttons for eyes along row of cheek shaping. Embroider mouth as illustrated. Stitch shoe laces with desired colour as illustrated.

Hair for both dolls: Evenly wind yarn for Hair lengthways around 21 cm (8 in) edge of cardboard until width of cardboard is covered, then cont to wind until desired thickness is reached. Cut off yarn. With chalk, mark a line across width at 8 cm (3 in) from one end. Slip yarn carefully off cardboard. Keeping the shape, put it into a thin plastic bag. With same colour cotton, sew along chalk line. Sew over line twice. Remove plastic bag. Place shorter looped end along forehead. Sew Hair onto head. Style and trim Hair as desired.

To finish Hansel's shorts: Sew inside leg seams. Sew crotch seam. Attach Straps at centre back. Cross Straps at back and take them over shoulders. Adjust length and sew a button on front end of Straps.

To finish Gretel's dress: Sew shoulder seams, including Sleeve sections. Sew press studs along back opening. With white yarn make a cord 56 cm (22 in) long. Thread cord through holes around waist and tie at back.

HINT

The simplest way to decrease a stitch is to work two stitches together. Unless the instructions indicate otherwise, do this one or two stitches in from the edge of your work. You can work up to three stitches together in this way, but no more. Some decreases such as on a raglan armhole are intended to be seen. In this case decrease by slipping the stitch on the right hand edge on to the right hand needle, knitting the next stitch and passing the slip stitch over it. At the other end, knit two stitches together.

HENRIETTA HIPPO

BODY
Work in st st. Beg at rear end, with A and 2 needles out of set of 4, cast on 10 sts. Work in st st, inc 1 st each end of 1st and every knit row until there are 20 sts, then work 11 rows straight ending with WS row. With 4 needles cont in rnds of st st as follows:

1st rnd: With RS facing, with 1st needle K20, with 2nd needle pick up 15 sts along side edge of piece to cast-on edge, cont to pick up 1 st from each of 1st 5 sts, (last st is centre top), with 3rd needle pick up 1 st from each of last 5 sts along cast-on edge, then cont to pick up 15 sts along side edge of piece. 60 sts.

Knit 1 rnd.
Divide for hindlegs
1st row: K8, leave 8 sts just worked on a piece of wool for Hindleg, K4 for crotch, TURN.

Cont on these 4 sts, beg with purl row work 9 rows in st st for crotch, break off. Slip these 4 sts onto a piece of wool.

With RS facing, rejoin A to next st from Crotch, K8. Slip these 8 sts just worked on a piece of wool for other hindleg. Cont to knit to end of rnd. 40 sts. Using 3 needles, working in rows and beg with purl row work

MATERIALS
Yarn: 8 ply pure new wool 50 g (2 oz) balls: 1¹/₂ balls pink (A); small quantity yellow (B)
Notions: Set of four 3.25 (3¹/₄) mm (No. 10) knitting needles; polyester fibre for filling; 2 small buttons for eyes; embroidery cotton

MEASUREMENTS
13 cm (5 in) high and 26 cm (10 in) long

SPECIAL ABBREVIATION
M1 = Make 1: insert right hand needle point from back of work and under horizontal loop before next st, lift it up, then insert left hand needle point in front loop of it and knit from this position

10 rows in st st, ending on a knit row.
Next rnd: With WS facing, with 1st needle, cast on 8 sts First of these 8 sts is beg of rnd.

With RS facing K4 over crotch piece, with WS facing cast on 8 sts, with RS facing and with 2nd needle K20, with 3rd needle K20. 60 sts. Place marker in first st of 1st needle to denote beg of rnd.
Always keep first st at beg of 1st needle. Knit 3 rnds.
Make top opening
1st row: K39, inc 1 st in next st, TURN.
2nd row: P60, inc 1 st in last st. 62 sts.
Working in rows cont in st st for 14 rows and end with WS row, TURN.
Divide for foreleg
Next row: K21, TURN.
Beg with purl row work 7 rows more in st st on these 21 sts only, TURN, knit 1 row and dec 1 st at end of the row, break off.
With RS facing, rejoin A to next st and K8. Slip these 8 sts just worked onto a piece of wool for foreleg. K4, TURN.
Beg with purl row work 9 rows more in st st on these 4 sts only. Break off and leave these 4 sts on a piece of wool.
Rep from ** to ** for other foreleg, K21, TURN.
Work 10 rows more in st st on these 21 sts only, and dec 1 st at end of last row, ending with RS row. With another needle, and with RS facing cont to K20 from next needle to complete rnd. Cont in rnds of st st as follows:
1st rnd: With 1st needle and with WS

facing, cast on 8 sts. First of these 8 sts is beg of rnd. With RS facing K4 from piece of wool, with WS facing cast on 8 sts, with 2nd needle K20, with 3rd needle K20. 60 sts. Work 4 rnds.
Shape neck
Keeping first st of rnd at beg of 1st needle, evenly dec 10 sts on next rnd, then on foll 2nd rnd once more. 40 sts. Work 2 rnds.
Next rnd: (K1 tbl) rep to end.
Work 2 rnds.
Shape head
Next rnd: K2, (M1, K4) rep to last 2 sts, M1, K2. 50 sts.
Work 2 rnds.
Next rnd: K2, (M1, K5) rep to last 3 sts, M1, K3. 60 sts.
Keeping first st of rnd at beg of 1st needle, rearrange sts evenly on 3 needles. Work 10 rnds.
Next rnd: Over 1st needle K20, over 2nd needle K8, (K2 tog) 6 times, over 3rd needle (K2 tog) 6 times, K8. There should be 20 sts on 1st needle and 14 sts each on 2nd and 3rd needles. Work 14 rnds.
Shape mouth
1st row: K1, slip this st onto end of 3rd needle, K18, slip these 18 sts onto a piece of wool for lower section of mouth, slip last st of 1st needle onto beg of 2nd needle, with 1st needle K23, sl1, K1, psso, TURN.
2nd row: Sl1 purlwise, P16, P2 tog, TURN.
3rd row: Sl1 knitwise, K16, sl1, K1, psso, TURN.
Rep 2nd and 3rd rows 4 times more, then 2nd row only once more, working all rem

18 sts onto one needle. Transfer other 18 sts from piece of wool onto another needle and graft sts tog or sew them tog.

LEGS

With RS facing and A, K8 from piece of wool. First st of these 8 sts is beg of rnd. With 2nd needle pick up 8 sts along side of Crotch piece then cont to pick up 4 sts to centre of cast-on edge, with 3rd needle pick up 4 sts over last half of cast-on edge, pick up 8 sts along side edge of work. 32 sts.

Keeping first st of rnd at beg of 1st needle work 12 rnds in A, change to B and work 2 rnds.

Shape sole

1st row: K8 and slip these 8 sts onto piece of wool, K15, sl1, K1, psso, TURN.

2nd row: Sl1 purlwise, P6, P2 tog, TURN.
3rd row: Sl1 knitwise, K6, sl1, K1, psso, TURN.

Rep last 2 rows 6 times, 2nd row once more, working rem 8 sts on one needle. Transfer other 8 sts from piece of wool to another needle and graft sts tog or sew them tog.

Work 3 other Legs in same way.

EARS

Make 2 each in A and B

With 2 needles, cast on 8 sts. Work in st st for 2 rows.

3rd row: K2, M1, K4, M1, K2. 10 sts.
Beg with purl row work 3 rows.

Dec row: K1, sl1, K1, psso, knit to last 3 sts, K2 tog, K1.

Work 1 row, then rep dec row once more, then cast/bind off purlwise.

TAIL

With A and 2 needles, cast on 15 sts, then cast/bind off immediately.

TO MAKE UP

Fill firmly and close opening, then rearrange filling for better shaping. Pair up Ear pieces with wrong sides tog, and using a fine backstitch and leaving cast-on edges open, sew around outer edge. Turn right side out. Fold lower edge in half and securely attach to head. Work same way for other Ear. Sew on buttons for eyes. With cotton, and chain stitch, embroider mouth, nostrils and hooves. Attach tail.

HERMAN THE TORTOISE

6-SIDED MOTIF FOR CENTRE

1st rnd: Wind black yarn twice round index finger of left hand for base loop, insert hook through base loop, yoh and draw a loop through. Keeping base loop firm with two fingers of left hand, work 3 ch and 11 tr in base loop. Draw up end of yarn tightly to close base loop. Drop black. With

white work sl st to top of 3 ch. 12 tr, counting 3 ch as 1 tr.

2nd rnd: With white, 1 ch, 1 dc in same place as sl st, (3 dc in next tr, 1 dc in next tr) rep to last dc, 3 dc in last tr.
Drop white. With black work sl st to 1st dc. 24 dc.

3rd rnd: With black, 1 ch, 1 dc in same dc as sl st, 1 dc in each dc to end. Drop black. With white work sl st to 1st dc.

4th rnd: With white, 1 ch, 1 dc in same dc as sl st, 1 dc in next dc, (3 dc in next dc, 1 dc in each of next 3 dc) rep to last 2 dc, 3 dc in next dc, 1 dc in last dc. Drop white. With black work sl st to 1st dc.

MATERIALS

Yarn: 8 ply pure new wool 50 g (2 oz) balls: 1 ball black; 1 ball white; 1½ balls yellow
Notions: One 3.50 (3½) mm (No. 9) crochet hook; polyester fibre for filling; black embroidery cotton

MEASUREMENTS

28 cm (11 in) long and 18 cm (7 in) wide

5th rnd: Work as 3rd rnd.
6th rnd: With white, 1 ch, 1 dc in same dc as sl st, 1 dc in each of next 2 dc, (3 dc in next dc, 1 dc in each of next 5 dc) rep to last 3 dc, 3 dc in next dc, 1 dc in each of last 2 dc. Drop white. With black work sl st to 1st dc. 48 dc.

7th rnd: With black, 1 ch, 1 dc in same dc as sl st, 1 dc in each of next 3 dc, *(1 dc, 2 ch, 1 dc) in next dc, 1 dc in each of next 7 dc, rep from * to last 4 dc, (1 dc, 2 ch, 1 dc) in next dc, 1 dc in each of last 3 dc, sl st to 1st dc, fasten off. There should be 9 dc between ch sps on each of 6 side edges.

5-SIDED MOTIFS

Make 6

1st rnd: Wind black yarn twice around index finger of left hand for base loop, insert hook in base loop, yoh and draw a loop through. Keeping base loop firm with two fingers of left hand, work 3 ch, then 9 tr in base loop. Draw up end of yarn tightly to close up base loop. Drop black. With white work sl st to top of 3 ch. 10 tr,

counting 3 ch as 1 tr.

Work as from 2nd to 7th rnds of 6-Sided Motif inclusively, taking note that there are 20 dc on 2nd rnd and 40 dc on 6th rnd.

BASE

1st rnd: Wind yellow yarn twice around Index finger of left hand for base loop, insert hook in base loop, yoh and draw a loop through. Keeping base loop firm with two fingers of left hand work 3 ch, then 14 tr in base loop. Draw up end of yarn tightly to close base loop, sl st to top of 3 ch. 15 tr, counting 3 ch as 1 tr.

2nd rnd: 3 ch, 1 tr in same place as sl st, 2 tr in each tr to end, sl st to top of 3 ch.

3rd rnd: 3 ch, 1 tr in same place as 3 ch, *1 tr in each of next 2 tr, 2 tr in next tr, rep from * to last 2 tr, 1 tr in each of last 2 tr, sl st to top of 3 ch.

4th rnd: 3 ch, 1 tr in same place as sl st, *1 tr in each of next 3 tr, 2 tr in next tr, rep from * to last 3 tr, 1 tr in each of last 3 tr, sl st to top of 3 ch.

5th rnd: 3 ch, work 1 tr in each tr to end AT SAME TIME evenly inc 10 tr on rnd, sl st to top of 3 ch. 60 tr.

6th rnd: 3 ch, 1 tr in same place as sl st. Work 1 tr in each tr AT SAME TIME work 2 tr in every foll 4th tr to end, sl st to top of 3 ch. 75 tr.

7th rnd: 3 ch, 1 tr in same place as sl st. Work 1 tr in each tr AT SAME TIME work 2 tr in every foll 5th tr to end, sl st to top of 3 ch.

8th rnd: Work as 5th rnd. 100 tr. Sl st to top of 3 ch, fasten off.

HEAD

With yellow, make 5 ch, 1 dc in 2nd ch from hook, 1 dc in each of next 2 ch, 3 dc in last ch, working on other side of foundation ch work 1 dc in each of next 2 ch, 2 dc in same place as 1st dc, sl st to 1st dc. 10 dc.

2nd rnd: 1 ch, 1 dc in each dc to end. Place marker in last dc of rnd to denote end of rnd and do not work sl st to join rnd.

3rd rnd: 1 ch, 1 dc in each dc AT SAME TIME inc 3 dc around each curve. Do not work sl st to join rnd.

Rep last 2 rnds once more. 22 dc.

Work 6 rnds more in dc in spiral as before, evenly dec 7 dc on next rnd. 15 dc rem.

Work 4 rnds more as before, sl st to next dc, fasten off.

LEGS

Make 4

With yellow, make 14 ch, sl st to 1st ch to form circle. Work in rnds of dc in spiral until there are 10 rnds from beg, sl st to next dc

then fold piece flat and work through all thickness as follows: 2 ch, (leaving last loop of each tr on hook work 1 tr in each of next 2 tr, yoh and draw through 3 loops on hook, 3 ch, sl st to base of last tr) 3 times but work last sl st to last dc instead of base of tr, fasten off.

TAIL

With yellow, make 10 ch, sl st to 1st ch to form circle, 1 ch, 1 dc in each of 10 ch, sl st to 1st dc, place marker in last dc.

Cont in rnds of dc in spiral without working sl st to join rnd. Work 4 rnds, evenly dec 2 dc on next rnd.

Work 2 rnds on rem 8 dc. On next rnd evenly dec 2 dc. Work 2 rnds more on rem 6 dc. Leaving a length of yarn, break off.

Thread end of yarn through rem 6 dc and draw tightly to form point.

TO MAKE UP

With wrong side of motifs tog and yellow yarn, join six of 5-Sided Motifs around 6-Sided Motif by working dc through all thicknesses. Join 5-Sides Motifs to each other at adjacent sides to form cup. Neatly join Base to cup by working dc through all thickness around outer edge and leaving an opening. Fill and close opening. Fill Head and attach in place. Fill Tail and attach in place. Fill Legs. Fold opening flat and close. Neatly attach Legs in position. With embroidery cotton and a wool sewing needle, stitch eyes and mouth.

CATERPILLARS

For two-tone caterpillar beg with A and alternate colours. For rainbow caterpillar use a different colour for each section.

With 2 needles and A, cast on 10 sts. Work in st st, inc 1 st each end of 3rd row and every foll 2nd row until 16 sts rem, then work 9 rows straight, dec 1 st each end of next row and every foll 2nd row until 10 sts rem, ending with RS row. Front section of face is made. Cont in rnds of st st as follows:

1st rnd: With RS facing, same needle and colour, pick up 5 sts along curve, 8 sts

MATERIALS

Yarn: For two-tone caterpillar: 5 ply pure new wool 50 g (2 oz) balls: 1/2 ball in each colour (A and B)

For rainbow caterpillar: 8 m long skeins tapestry wool: 3 skeins each of 6 different colours (A, B, C, D, E, F).

Notions: For both caterpillars: Set of four 3.25 (3^1/4) mm (No. 10) knitting needles; small quantity of another colour for hair; scrap of wool for mouth; polyester fibre for filling; 2 small beads for eyes; 3 small bells if desired – omit for children under 3 years

MEASUREMENTS

Approx 43 cm (17 in) long

down straight side edge. With 2nd needle pick up 5 sts on next curve, 10 sts on cast-on edge, 5 sts up next curve. With 3rd needle pick up 8 sts up straight side edge, 5 sts on next curve, then K5 from 1st needle. 56 sts.

Place marker in last st of 3rd needle to denote end of a rnd. This st is centre top of caterpillar. Cont in rnds for 22 rnds.

Eyelet rnd: K1, *K2 tog, yfwd, K2, rep from * to last 3 sts, K2 tog, yfwd, K1.

Knit 1 rnd, break off yarn. Head section is made.

**Join in next colour and knit 27 rnds. Work eyelet rnd, then knit 1 rnd. Break off yarn **.

Join in next colour and knit 4 rnds. Make opening as follows:

1st row: K56, TURN.
2nd row: P56, TURN.

Rep last 2 rows 8 times more, TURN, then with RS facing knit 5 rnds, then work eyelet rnd, then knit 1 rnd, break off yarn. Rep from ** to ** twice. Join in next colour and knit 20 rnds, then evenly dec 8 sts on next rnd and every foll 2nd rnd until 8 sts rem. Knit 1 rnd. break off, leaving a length of yarn. Thread end of yarn through rem sts, draw up tightly and securely fasten off.

EARS AND TAIL

With 2 needles and colour A, cast on 6 sts. Work in st st, inc 1 st each end of 1st, 3rd and 5th rows. 12 sts.

Work 7 rows straight, then dec 1 st each end of next and every foll 2nd row until 6 sts rem. Cast/bind off purlwise. Break off,

with a length of yarn attached. Make 3 in all. Thread end of yarn through sts around outer edge, draw up a little and fill to form a ball. Securely fasten off.

TO MAKE UP

Beg at top end, thread 4 strands of yarn for hair through eyelets around head section. Fill head firmly. Draw up 4 strands of yarn and, making 2.5 cm (1 in) long tassel at top, securely fasten off. Work same way for next section then cont to work in this way from Tail end until all sections are filled. Close opening. Securely attach 2 balls for Ears and 1 ball for Tail. Attach small bell on each Ear and Tail. Sew on small beads for eyes and stitch mouth.

KNITTING ABBREVIATIONS

alt = alternate; **beg** = begin/ning; **cm** = centimetre/s; **cont** = continue/ing; **dec** = decrease/ing; **foll** = following; **g st** = garter stitch; **g** = gram; **in** = inch/es; **incl** = including; **inc** = increase/ing; **K** = knit; **lp/s** = loop/s; **meas** = measure/ing; **0** = no stitches, rows or times; **patt** = pattern; **P** = purl; **psso** = pass the slip stitch over; **rem** = remain/ing; **rep** = repeat; **req** = required; **ret** = return; **rnd** = round; **RS** = right side; **RSF** = right side facing; **sl1** = slip one stitch; **sl st** = slip stitch; **st/s** = stitch/es; **st st** = stocking stitch; **tog** = together; **tbl** = through the back of the loop; **ybk** = yarn back from purl position to knit position; **yfwd** = yarn forward, bring yarn under needle and back to knit position creating a stitch; **yon** = yarn over needle; **yrn** = yarn around needle; **WS** = wrong side; **WSF** = wrong side facing.

CROCHET ABBREVIATIONS

Beg = begin/ning; **cm** = centimetres; **ch** = chain/s; **cont** = continue/ing; **dc** = double

crochet; **dec 1 st** = decrease 1 dc: (insert hook in next st, yoh and draw a loop through) twice; yoh and draw through 3 loops on hook; **dec 1 tr** = decrease 1 treble: (yoh, insert hook in next st, yoh and draw a loop through, yoh and draw through 2 loops on hook) twice, yoh and draw through 3 loops on hook; **h tr** = half treble;

in = inch/es; **inc** = increase; **patt** = pattern; **rem** = remain/ing; **rep** = repeat; **req** = required; **ret** = return; **rnd/s** = round/s; **RS** = right side; **sl st** = slip stitch; **sp/s** = space/s; **st/s** = stitch/es; **tog** = together; **yoh** = yarn over hook; **yrn** = yarn around hook; **WS** = wrong side